HELP ME PRAY

LEARNING
from the SAINTS

LOUISE PERROTTA

D1508831

SEI
BOOK

PUBLISHED BY ST. ANTHONY MESSENGER PRESS
CINCINNATI, OHIO

To my parents, Roger and Roma Bourassa,
who introduced me to both prayer and the saints

Unless otherwise noted, Scripture passages have been taken from the *Revised Standard Version,* Catholic edition. Copyright 1946, 1952, 1971 by the Division of Christian Education of the National Council of Churches of Christ in the USA. Used by permission. All rights reserved.

Cover design by Candle Light Studio
Cover images © Shutterstock
Book design by Mark Sullivan

LIBRARY OF CONGRESS CATALOGING-IN-PUBLICATION DATA
Help me pray : learning from the saints / [compiled by] Louise Perrotta.
p. cm.
Includes bibliographical references (p.   ).
ISBN 978-0-86716-973-7 (alk. paper)
1. Prayer—Catholic Church. 2. Christian saints—Quotations. I. Perrotta, Louise, 1946–
BV210.3.H457 2012
248.3'2—dc23
2011051740

ISBN 978-0-86716-973-7
Copyright ©2012, Louise Perrotta. All rights reserved.

Published by Servant Books, an imprint of
St. Anthony Messenger Press
28 W. Liberty St.
Cincinnati, OH 45202
www.AmericanCatholic.org
www.ServantBooks.org

Printed in the United States of America.
Printed on acid-free paper.

12 13 14 15 16 5 4 3 2 1

CONTENTS

· ❧ ·

INTRODUCTION

A *Little Help From Our Friends*

A large bookstore near my house hosts weekly discussion groups on topics such as writing, investing, travel, and, of course, books. A group was in full swing when I walked in one evening and found a seat at the coffee bar. Sipping my cappuccino directly across from where a dozen people were having a spirited exchange in American Sign Language, I began fantasizing: If I could gather anyone I chose into a discussion group, who would it be and what would we talk about?

Prayer, I decided in half a heartbeat. And in my mind's eye, I could almost picture that group sitting on folding chairs around the bookstore table. Mary and Joseph would be there. Teresa of Avila, John Chrysostom, Catherine of Siena, Abraham and David, Philip Neri, Francis de Sales, Elizabeth Seton, Mary of Bethany, Thérèse of Lisieux...

I don't really expect our local Barnes and Noble to be featuring an opportunity like this anytime soon. But while working on this book, I've come to see more clearly that in the Church there already exists an ongoing conversation about prayer, and I have come to see that we have access to it.

Scripture is our main point of entry, furnishing inexhaustible instruction on prayer and offering countless examples of men and women raising hearts and minds to God in every imaginable life situation. Because the Bible is God's *living* word, their stories have a unique power to draw us into the dialogue—addressing our hearts, eliciting our response, changing our lives.

God's Word had this effect on the saints, which is why their writings and lives can speak to us even over great divides of time and culture. Though not inspired in the same way as Scripture, the saints' words figure into the great live conversation on prayer. Rooted in God's living Word, their words are those of people who are gloriously alive and approachable in the communion of saints.

But if Scripture already contains all we need to know about prayer, why bother to approach the saints? From my own experience, four reasons spring immediately to mind:

Variety. If I hear enough different people speak about prayer in enough different ways, I just might start to get it.

Practical examples. I'm stimulated by seeing how the saints tried to live out Scripture—especially the parts that aren't spelled out, such as how to "pray constantly" (1 Thessalonians 5:17).

Encouragement. The saints had their weaknesses and their struggles with prayer, just as I do. They're credible advisors because they reveal what God can do in ordinary human beings who trust and never leave off talking to him. As St. André Bessette used to say, "What the Holy Spirit did for the apostles, he can do for us."

Prayer support. The saints aren't detached observers of my attempts to pray. They're a great "cloud of witnesses" (see Hebrews 12:1) cheering me on to the goal of union with God, with whom they're now united. On my own journey to God, I find assistance in both what the saints wrote in the past and what they pray about for me in the present.

In preparing this book, I've listened in on the saints' discussions with a view to collecting advice about "learning to pray." This is therefore not a guide for scaling the mystical heights. Neither does it cover all types of prayer—for example, the Eucharist and other forms of liturgical prayer. Having to choose just one aspect of a large reality, I've focused on the personal exchange that takes place when we follow Jesus' command to "go into your room and shut the door and pray to your Father who sees in secret" (Matthew 6:6).

I've addressed my questions mainly to the men and women whom the Catholic Church officially recognizes as saints or as candidates for canonization. A few members of the discussion are saints of the Orthodox Church. Some, like Thomas à Kempis and Br. Lawrence of the Resurrection, are not on the canonization track but produced writings that have led many Christians into lives of prayer.

On the reasonable assumption that you opened this book to seek guidance from the saints and not from me, I have tried to let the saints speak for themselves as much as possible. Except for short chapter introductions, this book consists of their contributions, roughly arranged according to subject.

Look through the table of contents and then dip into the book here and there or read chapter by chapter, according to your inclination. Linger over whatever catches your attention. Perhaps you'll find a thought to mull over or a saintly friendship to pursue. Ask your own questions about prayer, and know that what you'll find here is the tiniest sampling of what the saints have to say on the subject. Think of this collection as a mere chip from the richest of diamond mines, and be inspired to go digging for yourself. You'll find the sources for all quotes at the back of the book, in the notes section.

As I compiled this book, I thought often of an image suggested by Henry Suso, a fourteenth-century Dominican mystic. Whenever he was assailed by thoughts of his unworthiness, he imagined himself as a beggar positioned outside the door of a banquet hall where God was dining with his closest friends. As the privileged diners emerged, Henry saw himself addressing them "so that I might receive some small savor of their sweet fullness." Whenever he received so much as a word in return, said Henry, he was "as joyful as though I had found a treasure. I held it to me tenderly and said: 'Ah, sweet Lord, how I desire you. Shall I ever be able to say: You are mine and I am yours?'"

And this, I suggest, is the spirit in which we should approach this book. Let's allow our saintly friends' reflections and advice to lead us beyond conversation *about* prayer and deeper into that great conversation with God that is prayer itself.

CHAPTER ONE

Everyone's Invited

We love, Scripture says, because God first loved us (see 1 John 4:19). That's also why we pray—because God's love melts our chill, sparks our desire, ignites our love. The saints exemplify what happens to people who respond wholeheartedly to these divine initiatives: They are transformed, as sparks of love leap up into a great blaze of union with God.

Fortunately for those of us who are better described in terms of smoldering wicks or flickering flames, many saints wrote of their prayer life in a way that can encourage our own. One is the sixteenth-century Spanish Carmelite Teresa of Avila. Personable, practical, and profound, Teresa is a credible guide for spiritual strugglers because, by her own admission, she dabbled in prayer for almost two decades until a religious awakening prodded her on. Often during those years as a mediocre nun, she confides, "I was more occupied in wishing my hour of prayer were over, and in listening whenever the clock struck, than in thinking of things that were good."

To Teresa's astonishment, God didn't give up on her but kept calling gently. Once she got the message, he led Teresa to the heights of mystical prayer. "God is calling you, too," is her confident message to us. "Who can possibly despair, when he bore so long with *me?*"

Teresa is hardly condoning delay or halfheartedness. Calls from God require serious responses. Certainly, "there is no one for whom he makes it impossible to buy his riches," she says of the fruits of prayer. But "if you are to gain this, he would have you keep back nothing." And note this disarmingly simple but arduous piece of advice: "All that the beginner in prayer has to do…is to labor and be resolute and prepare himself with all possible diligence to bring his will into conformity with the will of God."

Calls and responses, commitments and resolutions—the following selections from Teresa and other saints touch on aspects of this dynamic of prayer. Never mechanical, it is at the very heart of intimacy with a loving God, who, Teresa asserts from experience, never fails to repay anyone who turns to him. "For mental prayer is nothing else, in my opinion, but being on terms of friendship with God, frequently conversing in secret with him who we know loves us."

Awakenings of Love and Desire

All through our life Christ is calling us. He called us first in Baptism; but afterwards also; whether we obey his voice or not, he graciously calls us still…. He calls us on from grace to grace, and from holiness to holiness, while life is given us….

It were well if we understood this; but we are slow to master the great truth, that Christ is, as it were, walking among us, and by his hand, or eye, or voice, bidding us follow him. We do not understand that his call is a thing which takes place now. We think it took place in the apostles' days; but we do not believe in it, we do not look out for it in our own case. We do not have eyes to see the Lord.

—*Bl. John Henry Newman*

This Lord of ours is so anxious that we should desire him and strive after his companionship that he calls us ceaselessly, time after time, to approach him; and this voice of his is so sweet....

His appeals come through the conversations of good people, or from sermons, or through the reading of good books; and there are many other ways.... Or they come through sicknesses and trials, or by means of truths that God teaches us at times when we are engaged in prayer; however feeble such prayers may be, God values them highly.

—*St. Teresa of Avila*

• • •

We are not drawn to God by iron chains, like bulls and wild oxen. We are drawn by enticements, sweet attractions, and holy inspirations....

Grace is so gracious, and so graciously seizes our hearts to draw them... that our free will suffers no violence.... How gently God handles our hearts! How skillfully he imparts his strength without interfering with our freedom.... He adjusts his power to his gentleness in such a way that when it comes to doing good, his might gently gives us power, while his gentleness maintains our freedom of will.

—*St. Francis de Sales*

• • •

Our good God waits for us patiently in our delays, he unceasingly calls us even though we don't answer him; he knocks at the very door of the heart that is shut to him....

When we feel urged to depart from a sin, to leave an imperfection, to correct a negligence, to grow in virtue, to make rapid strides to the perfection of divine love, then, the hour is come for us. Let us arise in haste, let us run to the divine Spouse, accept his grace, benefit by his inspiration; it is the hour of our deliverance; let us not delay, let us run!

—St. Jane Frances de Chantal

• • •

And anyone who has not begun to pray, I beg, for love of the Lord, not to miss so great a blessing. There is no place here for fear, but only desire.

—St. Teresa of Avila

• • •

Oh, eternal wisdom!… how skillfully you play the game of love; how well you can adapt yourself to the one you desire! Who else would woo his beloved as long as you do? Who would wait as patiently? Who else would remain as constant, in face of so many rebuffs, as you do, gentle, faithful, adorable Lord and Spouse of all loving souls? And because of all this, my own soul leans toward you, for you are the Good that—through its essential goodness—draws to itself all the ends of the earth….

Up, my children, the time has come!… Open the door, unlock your heart, let your lover enter, make up for the long time you have wasted by giving yourself to him in tender, devoted love.

—Bl. Henry Suso

• • •

"I do not play favorites," Christ told St. Catherine of Siena, "but I do respect holy desire, and I show myself in souls in proportion to the perfection with which they seek me." To Bl. Charles de Foucauld he said: "Prayer is primarily thinking of me with love—the more anyone loves me, the more he prays. Prayer is the attention of the soul lovingly fixed on me. The more loving that attention is, the better is the prayer."

• • •

Dorothy Day was in a common-law marriage, pregnant, a communist, and searching for God when she noted these stirrings of prayer in a 1925 diary entry:

I am surprised that I am beginning to pray daily. I began because I had to. I just found myself praying. I can't get down on my knees, but I can pray while I am walking. If I get down on my knees I think, "Do I really believe? Whom am I praying to?" And a terrible doubt comes over me, and a sense of shame, and I wonder if I am praying because I am lonely, because I am unhappy.

But when I am walking up to the village for the mail, I find myself praying again, holding the rosary in my pocket that Mary Gordon gave me in New Orleans two years ago. Maybe I don't say it right but I keep saying it because it makes me happy.

Then I think suddenly, scornfully, "Here you are in a stupor of content. You are biological. Like a cow. Prayer with you is like the opiate of the people....

"But," I reason with myself, "I am praying because I am happy, not because I am unhappy...."

And encouraged that I am praying because I want to thank him, I go on praying. No matter how dull the day, how long the walk seems, if I feel low at the beginning of the walk, the words I have been saying have insinuated themselves into my heart before I have done, so that on the trip back I neither pray nor think but am filled with exultation.

Choosing and Persevering

You will become holy if you desire it.

—*Bl. Marie of the Incarnation*

· · ·

Let us remember that God…has chosen never to put force upon our will. Let this be deeply impressed upon your heart: God in his love for us has desired to save us by his Son, but our salvation is not his will unless it is ours also.

—*St. Louise de Marillac*

· · ·

St. Teresa of Avila called prayer the royal road to heaven and stressed the importance of a good, resolute start for anyone who wants to travel it to the end.

How shall they begin? The most important thing, indeed, *the* important thing is for them to have a strong and resolute determination not to stop until they reach the sources of the living water.…They are determined to go forward, no matter what happens, despite all obstacles, all difficulties, all slander. They must say to themselves: I will keep going whether I reach the end of the journey or whether I die on the way, even if I do not have the courage to endure the difficulties I meet with, even if the world sinks under me! Often we are warned: "there is danger in that path"; "so-and-so was lost here"; "that person went astray"; "this one who prayed so much fell."

Pay no attention to the fears they may suggest to you or to the dangers they describe.… Do not let yourselves be deceived by anyone: there is but one road [to the fountain of living water]…and that is prayer.

• • •

Love to pray. Feel often during the day the need for prayer, and take trouble to pray. Prayer enlarges the heart until it is capable of containing God's gift of himself. Ask and seek, and your heart will grow big enough to receive him and keep him as your own.

—*Bl. Teresa of Calcutta*

• • •

He who perseveres to the end shall be saved. Piety must be habitual, not by fits. It must be persevering, because temptations continue all our life, and perseverance alone obtains the crown. Its means are the presence of God, good reading, prayer, the sacraments, good resolutions often renewed, the remembrance of our last ends.

—*St. Elizabeth Seton*

• • •

Dogged prayer reaches its goal. And if at the beginning prayer seems to you dry and stony, still from this hardest of rocks you will squeeze the oil of grace if only you persevere, if protracted delay does not sap your strength, if your longings do not grow slack from deferral. Deferral is obviously painful to a lover but desires prolonged grow stronger.

—*Gilbert of Hoyland*

• • •

In your spiritual ascent and your search after a closer union with God, you must not allow yourself to relax or slip back. But go forward till you have obtained the object of your desires. Follow the example of mountain climbers. If your desires turn aside after the objects which pass below, you will lose yourself in byways and countless distractions. Your mind will become dissipated and drawn in all directions by its desires. Your progress will be uncertain. You will not reach your goal, nor find rest after your labors.

But if your heart and mind, led on by love and desire, withdraw from the distractions of the world, you will grow strong. Your recollection will deepen the higher you rise on the wings of knowledge and desire....

Little by little as you abandon baser things to rest in the one true and unchangeable Good, you will dwell there, held fast by the bonds of love.

—*St. Albert the Great*

CHOICES MADE CONCRETE

The saints made practical resolutions about how to express and pursue their decision for Christ in their daily lives. Without slavishly imitating their lists, we can do the same. Here is one example, from Ven. Solanus Casey. These simple themes, jotted down in 1897, shortly after he entered the Capuchin seminary, became an integral part of his approach to God.

Means for Acquiring the Love of God

    I. Detachment of oneself from earthly affections. Singleness of purpose!

    II. Meditation on the Passion of Jesus Christ.

    III. Uniformity of will with the Divine Will.

    IV. Mental Prayer—meditation & contemplation.

    V. Prayer—Ask & it shall be given to you (Matthew 7:7).

• • •

Also in 1897, while on retreat in Nazareth, Bl. Charles de Foucauld noted some resolutions in the form of instructions given him by Christ:

Pay unceasing attention to me, and devote as long as possible to interior prayer and sacred reading, for they will make you one with me and through them I shall speak to you as I used to speak to my parents.... Base yourself on me. Lose yourself in me, immerse yourself in my love....

Never miss a possible moment, an instant, in the presence of the Blessed Sacrament.... The whole universe is nothing beside the Master of the universe who dwells in the tabernacle.

● ● ●

Dorothy Day, a woman noted for her active promotion of social justice, made these resolutions to keep herself focused on God in the midst of her busy life:

"Can you not watch one hour with me [Mark 14:37]."

I shall remember this whenever I am tired and want to omit prayer, the extra prayers I shall set myself....

Morning prayers, in my room before going to Mass. I always omit them, rushing out of the house just in time as I do. If I were less slothful it would be better....

Around the middle of the day to take, even though it be to snatch, fifteen minutes of absolute quiet, thinking about God and talking to God.

Read the Office as much as I can....

One visit [to the Blessed Sacrament] during the day, always without fail.

Rosary daily.

I do plenty of spiritual reading to refresh myself and to encourage myself so I do not have to remind myself of that.

The thing to remember is not to read so much or talk so much about God, but to talk to God.

To practice the presence of God.

To be gentle and charitable in thought, word and deed. (Most important of all.)

• • •

Elisabeth Leseur, married to a loving but militantly atheistic doctor, suffered from hepatitis for much of her life. In 1911, the year she was diagnosed with cancer, she made these practical resolutions:

To fast: spiritually, by more constant efforts with myself and sacrifices and suffering; physically by self-denial in food, by privations and all my bodily misery.

To pray: by confession, more fervent Communions, meditation on the Passion, visits to the Blessed Sacrament, the rosary, the penitential psalms, the Way of the Cross; by sermons and pious exercises, by more constant and peaceful union of my soul with God.

Almsgiving: Of a little money, but also of my time, my heart, my prayers and my suffering. To have a boundless charity in my heart—sweet, tender, strong, always active and including everyone, especially people who don't attract me.

To become humbler, more silent about myself. . . . Not to look dejected, not to carry human dissatisfactions as if they were a heavy burden, but to let my joy shine on all, the fruit of renunciation and penance.

• • •

Reflect upon the everlasting love God has had for you…. He has always loved you from all eternity, and for this reason he has prepared for you all these graces and favors…. Among other things, he has thought of enabling you to make your resolutions to serve him….

Beloved resolutions, you are the fair tree of life that God with his own hand has planted within my heart, the tree my Savior desires to water with his blood and thus make fruitful!… O fair and holy resolutions, if I keep you, you will keep me; if you live in my soul, my soul will live in you.

Live then forever, resolutions which are everlasting in the mercy of my God! Live eternally in me, and let me never forsake you!

—*St. Francis de Sales*

CHAPTER TWO

A Few Good Habits

"If you are careful to form habits of the kind I have mentioned, you will derive such great profit from them that I could not describe it even if I wished." The voice is Teresa of Avila's; the "habits" are basic disciplines of prayer—things like showing up regularly and focusing. Each in his or her own way, all the saints cultivated these disciplines, establishing habits and priorities that served as openings to grace.

St. Teresa Benedicta of the Cross (Edith Stein), who converted to Catholicism in 1921 after reading the autobiography of St. Teresa of Avila, took the advice of the Carmelite mystic seriously. Edith discovered the benefits of healthy routine early in life. She was raised in a devout Jewish home where religious customs and traditions were faithfully observed. A disciplined scholar, she developed into an outstanding philosopher. In 1933 she entered the Carmelites, embracing a structured prayer life that included daily Mass, the Divine Office, and two hours of meditation.

It all came to an end in August 1942, when the Nazis arrested Edith and her sister Rosa. The two women were taken to Auschwitz and gassed.

For more than ten years before her entry into religious life, Edith was a brilliant lay professional who taught, wrote, and lectured widely. From experience, she knew how challenging it can be to balance daily commitments and give God priority. This is why, in a 1932 lecture, she insisted on each Christian's responsibility to select some prayer practices and shape them into a flexible "plan for daily and yearly living...in order to make ready the way for the Lord."

Edith offered as a concrete suggestion the following approach for beginning a busy day. Like the best advice of the saints on prayer, it is practical and realistic.

· · ·

The duties and cares of the day ahead crowd about us when we awake in the morning, if they have not already dispelled our night's rest. Now arises the uneasy question: How can all this be accommodated in one day? When will I do this, when that? How shall I start on this and that? Thus agitated, we would like to run around and rush forth. We must then take the reins in hand and say, "Take it easy!... My first morning's hour belongs to the Lord. I will tackle the day's work which he charges me with, and he will give me the power to accomplish it...."

So I will go to the altar of God [to Mass]....Then I may ask him, "Lord, what do you want of me?" And after quiet dialogue, I will go to that which I see as my next duty.

MAKE ROOM FOR GOD

The biggest challenge many of us face in our prayer lives is finding time and a quiet place to hear God. The saints dealt with this challenge, too. They encourage us to make time with God our top priority.

A little sprinkling of water which merely settles the dust and dampens the surface is useless for enriching the soil; plenty of water is needed....

In the same way, we need an abundance of heavenly dew and water if we are to bring forth the fruit of good works. With good reason, then, we are advised to take as much time for prayer as we can.... Often enough, it takes us half an hour just to quiet our mind and tune our instrument, so to speak....

But whoever is pressed for time on account of many duties should keep offering his little coin, like the poor widow in the temple. If no negligence is involved, God, who provides for all created things according to their needs and nature, will provide for this need too.

—*St. Peter of Alcantara*

• • •

We ought to have fixed hours of prayer.

—*St. Jerome*

• • •

If you avoid unnecessary talk and aimless visits, listening to news and gossip, you will find plenty of suitable time to spend in meditation on holy things.

—*Thomas à Kempis*

• • •

St. Alphonsus Liguori stressed the importance of finding a quiet place for personal prayer and especially recommended visits to the Blessed Sacramaent.

St. Teresa said that in this world it is impossible for all subjects to speak to the king. As for the poor, the most they can hope for is to speak with him by means of some third person. But to speak with you, O King of heaven, there is no need of third persons; for everyone that wishes can find you in the Most Holy Sacrament, and can speak to you at his pleasure and without restraint....

Oh how Jesus seems to continually exclaim from the altar: "Come to me, all you who labor and are burdened, and I will give you rest" (Matthew 11:28). Come, he says, come, you poor; come, you infirm; come, you afflicted; come, you just and you sinners, and you shall find in me a remedy for all your losses and afflictions. Such is the desire of Jesus Christ: to console everyone who has recourse to him, he remains day and night on our altars, that he may be found by all and that he may bestow favors upon all.

—*St. Alphonsus Liguori*

PRAYER'S DAILY RHYTHMS

St. Vincent de Paul gave this advice to some Sisters of Charity in 1640. It's helpful for anyone who wants to start the day with God.

Rise punctually…. The whole order of the day depends on this first action. You must acquire this habit courageously…. Our bodies are like donkeys—accustomed to one road, they will always follow it. To make this habit easy, make it a rule to go to bed at the right time….

Always do what you can to make prayer your first occupation so that your mind may be filled with God for the rest of the day.

• • •

In his Introduction to the Devout Life, *St. Francis de Sales gives a four-point instruction on beginning each day.*

1. Thank and adore God wholeheartedly for the blessing of having been kept alive by him during the night. If you fell into any sin in the course of it, ask his forgiveness.

2. Realize that the present day has been given you so that through it you may win the coming day of eternity. Make a firm resolution to use the day well for this purpose.

3. Think ahead to the work, contacts, and other opportunities for serving God that you might encounter during the day. Foresee which temptations might arise to lead you into sin, whether through anger, pride, or some other lack of self-control. Prepare yourself by making a holy resolution to use well all the means you will be offered to serve God and advance in devotion; likewise, resolve to avoid, fight, and conquer whatever might arise to oppose your salvation and God's glory....

4. Humble yourself before God, acknowledging that by yourself you can carry out none of your plans.... As if you were holding your heart in your hands, offer it to God with all its good intentions. Implore him to take it into his protection and strengthen it for success in his service.... Ask Our Lady, your guardian angel, and the saints to help you in all this.

• • •

Our morning offering...seals the whole day.... If it is made fully and sincerely—even though we should forget to renew it from hour to hour as we commonly do, and not retract it by any act of our will—and if no mortal sin comes in the way, our first good offering secures all we do for the day. What a comfort that is!

—*St. Elizabeth Seton*

• • •

During the activities of the day,...unite your will to God's by confirming your morning resolution. Do this either by a simple, loving glance at God, or by a few words spoken quietly.... "Yes, Lord, I want to do this action because you want it," or simply, "Yes, Father," or, "O Holy Will, live and rule in me," or other words that the Holy Spirit will suggest to you. You may also make a simple sign of the cross over your heart.... All this will show that above everything, you want to do the holy will of God and seek nothing but his glory in all that you do.

—*St. Jane Frances de Chantal*

• • •

St. Teresa Benedicta of the Cross recommended breaking up a busy workday with periodic breathing spaces for turning to the Lord.

Each one must know, or get to know, where and how she can find peace. The best way, when it is possible, is to shed all cares again for a short time before the tabernacle.... And when no outer rest whatever is attainable, when there is not place in which to retreat, if pressing duties prohibit a quiet hour, then at least she must for a moment seal off herself inwardly against all other things and take refuge in the Lord. He is indeed there and can give us in a single moment what we need.

• • •

"By the morning exercise, you open the windows of your soul to the Sun of Justice," says St. Francis de Sales. "By the evening exercise, you close them to the darkness of hell." A bedtime "examination of conscience" is indispensable. "Everyone knows how it should be done," he says, and then spells it out anyway:

1. We thank God for having protected us during the day.

2. We examine how we behaved in the course of the day. To make this easier, we think about where we were, with whom, and what we were doing.

3. If we find that we did something good, we thank God for it. On the other hand, if we discover that we sinned in thought, word, or deed,

we ask God's forgiveness, resolving to mention this in Confession at the earliest opportunity and to diligently change our ways.

4. We then entrust to Providence our body and soul, the Church, relatives, and friends. We ask Our Lady, our guardian angel, and the saints to watch over us and for us. With God's blessing, we go to take the rest he ordained that we need.

SPECIAL PRAYER TIMES AND SEASONS

While prayer is a daily encounter with God, the saints also recognized particular seasons, days, and even moments of his grace.

Sunday is the property of our good God; it is his own day, the Lord's day. He made all the days of the week. He might have kept them all. He has given you six and has reserved only the seventh for himself.

—*St. John Vianney*

• • •

St. Bernadette saw the moments after receiving Holy Communion as a most precious time of prayer. "How do you manage to remain so long at your thanksgiving?" a nun asked her one day. Bernadette replied: "I think to myself that the Blessed Virgin is giving me the Infant Jesus, I welcome him, I speak to him, and he speaks to me."

• • •

The Catholic liturgy has a great attraction for me; I love to live the great communal life of the church in the course of the year, uniting myself with its joys and sorrows, joining my poor prayers with its prayers, my weak voice with its strong voice. It is consoling to go through the liturgical cycle, living our Savior's life, from his incarnation to his death and ascension; through the words of the prophets, fathers, and saints of all ages to speak my faith and my love; to adore him in company with those who have adored him through the centuries; to offer myself with shepherds, disciples, and martyrs with people from all times, to feel myself living in the great Catholic communion, after so many others, and before so many who will follow me, with my homage to the infant God, the suffering Christ, the risen Lord.

—Elisabeth Leseur

• • •

Sometimes the liturgical cycle—or the cycle of events in one's own life—is occasion for taking a spiritual retreat.

Servants of God ought to set aside a fixed time in which to devote themselves to prayer. In addition to this ordinary and daily exercise, they should at times withdraw completely from every kind of occupation, however holy, in order to concentrate on spiritual exercises....This may be done at any time, but especially for the principal feasts of the year, in periods of trouble and distress, or after a long journey or any absorbing business which may have led to distraction and dissipation of heart.

—St. Peter of Alcantara

• • •

A retreat is to the whole of life what meditation is to a day. The soul gathers new strength and resumes the daily duty changed and sanctified. Giving myself is easier when my soul has been replenished.

—Elisabeth Leseur

THE DISCIPLINE OF SOLITUDE

You know how, before beginning his public life, Jesus retired in prayer for forty days in the desert. You too try to bring *a little silence* into your lives, so as to be able to think, to reflect, to pray with greater fervor and make resolutions with greater decision.

It is difficult to create "zones of desert and silence" these days, because you are continually being overcome by the complications of your work, the uproar of events, the attraction of the communications media, so much so that inner peace is compromised.... It is difficult, but it is possible and important to know how to succeed in it.

You too can put aside a little time, in the evening especially, for praying, for meditating, for reading a page of the Gospel or an episode in the life of some saint. Create a zone of desert and silence for yourself in that way.

—*Bl. John Paul II*

• • •

It is spiritual solitude that the Lord Christ requires of you, though bodily withdrawal is not without its uses when it may be had, especially in time of prayer. You have his own commandment in the matter: "When you pray, enter into your room..." (Matthew 6:6). He himself practiced what he preached: he would spend all night in prayer, not only hiding from the crowds but not allowing any even of his closest friends to come with him....You must do likewise when you want to pray.

Be quite clear that the only solitude required of you is that of mind and spirit. You are alone in spirit if you are not thinking about ordinary matters, if you are not interested in things present, if you reject worldly values, if you keep out of quarrels, if you do not resent injuries or hug grievances. Otherwise you are not really alone, even when you are alone in body. Do you see that it is possible both to be alone in a crowd, and to be in a crowd when you are alone? No matter how many people there may be around you, you are alone, if only you do not pry eagerly into their conversation or judge it harshly.

—*St. Bernard of Clairvaux*

• • •

Silence is the great master. It speaks to the human heart. Silence is not an empty void; God dwells therein.

—*Père Jacques (Lucien-Louis Bunel)*

• • •

St. Thomas More took to heart the contrast between Jesus, who often spent his nights "praying under the open sky," and "the hypocritical Pharisee…snoring away in his soft bed."

How I wish that those of us who are prevented by our own laziness from imitating the illustrious example of our Savior might at least be willing to call to mind his all-night vigils when we turn over on the other side in our beds, half asleep, and that we might then, during the short time before we fall asleep again, offer him thanks, condemn our slothfulness, and pray for an increase of grace. Surely if we set out to make a habit of doing even the least little bit of good, I feel certain that God will set us forward a great way on the path of virtue.

• • •

Blessed are the nights which God allows me to spend in intimate conversation with him. My Lord and my God, let me realize the value of such moments as much as I should…. Teach me to extend those hours where I keep solitary vigil at your feet while the world slumbers….

Our Lady of Perpetual Help, I have never prayed to you in vain.…
Keep your hand on me to prevent me from sleeping at Jesus' feet, as I
unfortunately do so often when he invites me to pray to him and with
him, to spend an hour alone with him.

—*Bl. Charles de Foucauld*

JUST DO IT!

What wife is there who would not give her husband at least a ring…
as a mark of her love and an assurance that she will be his until death?
Does our Lord, then, deserve less, that we should mock him by giving
and then taking back the trifle we gave him? But this little bit of time
we decide to give him out of all the time we spend on ourselves and on
others,…let us give…with a firm determination never to take it back,
[considering it] as something that no longer belongs to us.

—*St. Teresa of Avila*

• • •

Let us confess our shortcomings to God and on no account abandon
diligence in prayer. For it is better to be blamed for frequent omissions
than for complete neglect.

—*St. Mark the Ascetic*

CHAPTER THREE

A Question of Attitude

In prayer, as in the rest of life, it's possible to spoil a good thing by approaching it with the wrong attitude. Spiritual writers over the centuries have therefore stressed the importance of coming to prayer with the right spirit—with, among other things, humility, faith, reverence, and love.

Bl. Columba Marmion gave a simple explanation of these foundational attitudes by contrasting two scriptural figures who illustrate opposing approaches. On one side is the "praying" Pharisee of Jesus' parable, who proudly calls God's attention to his supposed superiority and great achievements: "I fast twice a week, I give tithes of all that I get" (Luke 18:12). "God detests such self-righteous people, though they may be very correct and irreproachable," Abbot Marmion observed.

On the other side is St. Paul, who refused to pride himself on his accomplishments. His attitude was *I see my own righteousness as nothing. My confidence is in Jesus, who alone gives value to what I do* (see Philippians 3:4–11; 2 Corinthians 11:30; 12:9). St. Paul takes pride in his weaknesses and not in his works, said Marmion. People like him are "dear to God because they glorify his Son."

Confidence in God and clear-sighted humility—while these attitudes characterize every saint's prayer life, they are especially obvious in St.

Thérèse of Lisieux, who made them the centerpiece of her "little way" to holiness. She called not for great works but for doing life's ordinary tasks with great love and joyful trust. Her way, said St. Thérèse, was like "an elevator to carry me to Jesus, for I was too small to climb the steep stairs of perfection." Meditating on Jesus' welcome of little children, Thérèse rejoiced in her littleness. To her mind it was a positive advantage, proof of her claim on God's mercy: "The elevator which must raise me to heaven is your arms, O Jesus!" Becoming great is not the goal here. "In fact, just the opposite: I must become less and less."

Each in his or her own way, Columba Marmion, Thérèse, and all the saints encourage us to ground our prayer in the self-knowledge that leads to true humility and hope in God. These are the attitudes explored in this chapter. Essentially, they revolve around two questions: Who is God? Who am I?

The saints' answers to these two questions drew them into intimacy with God. We might ask ourselves: Where are our answers drawing us?

THE GREAT DISCREPANCY

The confessor of St. Catherine of Siena described the following experience as the solid foundation for Catherine's life of union with Christ and said it contained a truth of "immeasurable wisdom":

When the Lord Jesus Christ first began to appear to her, he once came to her while she was praying and said, "Do you know, daughter, who you are, and who I am? If you know these two things, you will be blessed. You are she who is not.... I AM he who is. Have this knowledge in your soul and the enemy will never deceive you and you will escape all his wiles. You will never disobey my commandments and will acquire all grace, truth, and light."

—*Bl. Raymond of Capua*

• • •

Spying on St. Francis of Assisi at prayer one moonlit night, his friend Br. Leo found him lying face up, arms outstretched in a cross, repeating over and over: "O dearest Lord and God, what are you? And what am I, your little useless worm of a servant?" Later, asked for an explanation, Francis said: "In that prayer you heard, two lights were manifested to me: one light in which I knew the Creator, and one in which I knew myself…. I saw the infinite depth of the divine Godhead and my own wretched abyss of misery. And so I said, 'What are you, Lord, the highest, the wise, the all-good, the all-merciful, that you trouble yourself about me?'"

• • •

Try this exercise to get an idea of just how stupid it is to ignore the gap between God's greatness and your sinfulness, suggests St. Thomas More. Picture yourself as a criminal guilty of high treason. You're headed for execution when the prince, who is inclined to mercy, gives you an audience with him—a chance for freedom, if only you demonstrate a change of heart. Now, imagine yourself throwing that chance away by taking a careless, cavalier approach to the meeting.

While he stays in one place and listens attentively, stroll around here and there as you run through your plea. Then, when you have had enough of walking up and down, sit down on a chair, or if courtesy seems to require that you condescend to kneel down, first command someone to come and place a cushion beneath your knees…. Then yawn, stretch, sneeze, spit without giving it a thought, and belch up the fumes of your gluttony. In short, conduct yourself in such a way that he can clearly see...that while you are addressing him you are thinking about something else....

Certainly we would consider it quite mad to defend ourselves in this way before a mortal prince against a charge that carries the death penalty.... And do we think it is reasonable to beg pardon so contemptuously from the King of all kings?

• • •

Why has [God] loved me so much? I feel so little, so full of misery, but I love him; that is all I know how to do, I love him with his own love, it is a double current between he who is and she who is not! Ah, when I feel God invade my whole soul, as I pray to him for you, it seems to me that it is a prayer he cannot resist, and I want him to make me all-powerful!

—Bl. Elizabeth of the Trinity

• • •

On March 24, 1620, as Bl. Marie of the Incarnation was walking to work and praying about her business affairs, she had a mystical insight into God's love and her own sinfulness that changed her forever.

In a flash the eyes of my mind were opened and all the faults, sins, imperfections I had ever committed were represented to me both in general and in particular, with a distinction and clarity more certain than any certitude that human effort could produce. At the same moment I saw myself completely immersed in blood, and I was convinced that it was the blood of the Son of God...and that this precious blood had been shed for my salvation.

If the goodness of God had not sustained me, I believe I would have died of fright, so horrible and shocking is the sight of sin, however small it may be. No human tongue can express it…. But to see not only the fact of one's personal culpability but also the fact that, even if one were the only one guilty of the sin, the Son of God would have done for him what he has done for all…. In this same moment my heart felt snatched from itself and transformed into his love…and the experience of this love begot in me the most intense sorrow and regret for having offended him….

I returned to our home changed into another person, but so powerfully changed that I didn't know myself any more. I saw unmasked my ignorance which had caused me to believe that I was quite perfect, that my actions were innocent, and finally that all was well with me; but now I humbly confessed that my justices were but iniquities.

THE GLORY IN WEAKNESS

We must always live in the knowledge that we can do nothing by our own strength. We will then be imitating St. Philip Neri, who used to say to God every morning upon awakening, "My Jesus, if you do not keep your hand on Philip this day, he is sure to betray you."

• • •

This is all the grand science of Christians: to know that we are nothing and can do nothing of ourselves…. Then we will never neglect to seek through prayer that strength which we do not have on our own and which we need in order to resist temptation and do good. And so with the help of God, who never refuses anything to those who pray to him in humility, we will be able to do all things.

—*St. Alphonsus Liguori*

• • •

If you were at the point of death, what thought would give you confidence about standing before God's judgment seat to give an account of your life? Here's what St. Claude de la Colombière said would help him:

It would be nothing other than the number and greatness of my sins. Here is a confidence really worthy of God: far from allowing us to be depressed by the sight of our faults, it strengthens us…by its infinite conception of the goodness of our Creator.

• • •

Our imperfections should not please us…, but on the other hand they should not dismay or discourage us. We should rather make them a cause for submission, humility, and being on our guard against self; but not for discouragement or affliction of heart, and even less for a lack of confidence in God's love for us; for though it is true that God does not love our imperfections and venial sins, he loves us very much in spite of them. Thus a child's weakness and infirmity does not please a mother but she nevertheless goes on loving her child, even tenderly and with compassion….

Live joyfully. Our Lord's eyes are on you and he is looking at you lovingly, all the more tenderly because you are so helpless. Never allow your will to foster contrary thoughts; and when they beset you, do not look at them in themselves, turn your eyes away from their iniquity, and turn towards God with brave humility, speaking to him about his ineffable goodness which makes him love our poor, feeble and abject human nature in spite of its infirmities.

—*St. Francis de Sales*

• • •

Always turn your eyes from the study of your own sin to the contemplation of God's mercy. Devote much more thought to the grandeur of his love for you than to your unworthiness towards him, to his strength than to your weakness. When you have done this, surrender yourself into God's arms in the hope that he will make you what he requires you to be and that he will bless all you do.

—*St. Vincent de Paul*

• • •

Ven. Solanus Casey, writing to a woman who had asked his spiritual counsel:

Your failure, yes, is an indication of weakness of some kind, somewhere. But if "the weak thing[s] of this world hath God chosen to confound the strong…," as St. Paul so wonderfully assures us…[1 Corinthians 1:27], then why ever be discouraged…?

Why, dear sister, you ought to rather thank God for having given you such an opportunity to humble yourself and such a wonderful chance to foster humility—and by thanking him ahead of time for whatever crosses he may deign to caress you with, [having] CONFIDENCE in his wisdom. Confidence in God—the very soul of prayer—hardly comes to any poor sinner like we all are without trials and humiliations….There is a little verse I am sure will profit you to keep in mind and ought [to] help you foster confidence in God: *"God condescends to use our powers if we don't spoil his plans by ours."* God's plans are always for the best, always wonderful. But most especially for the patient and the humble who trust in him are his plans unfathomably holy and sublime.

• • •

The moment of outdoor prayer that St. Elizabeth Seton describes here took place in 1789, when she was fifteen.

I set off to the woods about a mile from home and soon found an outlet to a meadow, and a chestnut tree attracted my attention, and when I came to it I found rich moss at the foot. There then was a soft seat; the sun was warm, the air still, a clear blue vault above; and all around I heard the numberless sounds of the joy and melody of spring. The sweet clover and wild flowers I had gathered by the way were in my hand. I was filled with love of God and admiration, enthusiastic even, of his works....

God was my Father, my all. I prayed, sang hymns, cried, laughed, talking to myself of how far he could place me above all sorrow. There I lay still to enjoy the heavenly peace that came over my soul, and I am sure, I grew, in the two hours so passed, ten years in my spiritual life.

• • •

If only we could say in utter truth these words, "My God is my all," we would never find our prayer long or boring. When boredom descended upon us in prayer, that simple phrase said from the heart would act like a spell to drive away our weariness and disgust.

—*St. Jane Frances de Chantal*

ASK FORGIVENESS AND MERCY

I come to your feet, most loving Father. Behold, my sins have made a separation between you and me. Ah! Have mercy on me according to the multitude of your mercy, break down the wall of my old way of life which keeps me from you; and draw me so vehemently toward you that I may, in the gentleness of your inextinguishable cherishing-love, wisely follow you by loving.

Lovingly kind Jesus, although the will [to do what is good] is in me, I do not find [the strength] to accomplish it. Therefore turn my soul from the frailty of the human condition toward you in such a way that I may untiringly run in the way of your commandments and cling inseparably to you.

—*St. Gertrude the Great*

• • •

You are here in me, my God.

And before you, in you, morning to evening, at every moment,

I commit imperfections, sins without number in thought, word, and deed.

I'm terrified. I'm tempted to say, "Depart from me, Lord, for I am a sinner."

But I don't say it.

No, on the contrary:

"Stay with us, Lord, for night is falling."

I am in the night of sin, and the light of salvation cannot come to me except through you.

Stay, Lord, for I am a sinner.

—*Bl. Charles de Foucauld*

GIVE THANKS

Let us thank God at all times and under whatever circumstances. Thank him for our creation and our existence. Thank him for everything—for his plans in the past that by our sins and our want of appreciation and patience have so often been frustrated and that he so often found necessary to change. Let us thank him for all his plans for the future—for trials and humiliations as well as for great joy and consolations; for sickness and whatever death he may deign to plan.

Therefore we should thank him frequently for not only the blessings of the past and present, but thank him ahead of time for whatever he foresees is pleasing to him that we suffer.

—*Ven. Solanus Casey*

• • •

Know that gratitude for God's benefits is one of the riches of the soul, and that ingratitude dries up the fountain of divine graces. Give your tribute of gratitude often to the most loving Jesus. Often look back over your lives and consider the graces…that you have received. If you meditate well, you will perceive the torrents of these saving waters of divine grace which have poured into your soul at the various stages and circumstances of your lives.

—*St. Frances Cabrini*

• • •

Give thanks to God "in all circumstances" (1 Thessalonians 5:18)—but do so in a way that honors him, warns St. Bernard of Clairvaux, for "even the Pharisee gives thanks" (see Luke 18:11).

Do you not perceive that the Pharisee, in offering thanks, honors God with his lips but in his heart pays tribute to himself? And so, through force of habit more than by intention or inclination, you will hear people of all sorts pronouncing words of thanks, for even the wickedest persons will offer a perfunctory thanks to God…when their perverse will was fulfilled.

For instance, when the thief has bagged the loot for which he has planned, he celebrates in the privacy of his hide-out and says: "Thank God! I have not watched in vain, the night's work has not been wasted." The murderer will brag and express his thanks for the overthrow of a rival, for having had revenge on an enemy. And the adulterer will utter an irreverent "Thank you, God," as he capers with delight on having gone to bed at last with the woman he has long pursued.

It is clear then that God will listen only to the thanks that spring from a pure and genuine simplicity of heart.

ASK AND INTERCEDE

John Damascene says that "to pray is to ask fitting things of God." It often happens that our prayers are not granted because we ask for that which is not good for us: "You ask and do not receive, because you ask wrongly" (James 4:3).

It is no easy matter to know what we should pray for, since it is difficult to know what we ought to desire.... For this reason the apostle Paul says that "we do not know how to pray as we ought" (Romans 8:26).

Now Christ is our teacher.... Therefore, his disciples said to him, "Lord, teach us to pray" (Luke 11:1). It follows, then, that we pray most rightly when we ask for what he taught us to pray for. Consequently, Augustine says, "If we would pray rightly and fittingly, we should say nothing else but what is contained in this prayer of our Lord."

—St. Thomas Aquinas

• • •

I can state quite briefly what you ought to pray for: Pray for a happy life…. Perhaps you ask, "What is a happy life?"…The person who is truly happy is the one who has all that he wishes to have, and wishes to have nothing which he ought not to wish.

—*St. Augustine*

• • •

St. Catherine of Siena's great spiritual work, The Dialogue, *opens with a third-person reference to herself as "a soul" who presents the Father with four requests—only one of them for herself.*

A soul rises up, restless with tremendous desire for God's honor and the salvation of souls…..

Now this soul's will was to know and follow truth more courageously. So she addressed four petitions to the most high and eternal Father, holding up her desire for herself first of all—for she knew that she could be of no service to her neighbors in teaching or example or prayer without first doing herself the service of attaining and possessing virtue….

The second was for the reform of holy Church. The third was for the whole world in general…. In her fourth petition she asked divine providence to supply…for a certain case which had arisen [perhaps a criminal awaiting execution, or a priest struggling with despair.]

• • •

St. Faustina Kowalska heard Jesus speak these words to her during a retreat just before Pentecost 1938:

"My daughter, know that my heart is mercy itself. From this sea of mercy, graces flow out upon the whole world…. My daughter, I desire that your heart be an abiding place of my mercy. I desire that this mercy flow out upon the whole world through your heart. Let no one who approaches you go away without that trust in my mercy which I so ardently desire for souls.

"Pray as much as you can for the dying. By your entreaties, obtain for them trust in my mercy, because they have most need of trust, and have it the least.... You know the whole abyss of my mercy, so draw upon it for yourself and especially for poor sinners. Sooner would heaven and earth turn into nothingness than would my mercy not embrace a trusting soul."

SIMPLE WORDS

You don't need to use many or high-sounding words. Just repeat often, "Lord, show me your mercy as you know best." Or "God, come to my assistance."

—*St. Macarius the Great*

• • •

St. Peter Julian Eymard, who founded two religious orders dedicated to the Eucharist and to adoration of the Blessed Sacrament, suggested these conversation topics for a Holy Hour with Jesus:

Speak to him of himself, of his heavenly Father, of all that he has done for his Father's glory; this will gladden his heart. Speak to him of his love for men and women; this will fill his heart and yours with happiness. Speak to him of his mother, and you will be praising his filial affection. Speak to him of all the saints; this will glorify his divine grace in them.

Jesus...will then speak to you about yourself. Under the influence of this conversation, your heart will be filled with peace and joy.... In silence and rest you will hear Jesus' gentle voice penetrating your soul. Not only that—your very silence and stillness will be transformed into the highest activity of love: *You will become one with him.*

What most hinders the action of grace in our souls is the fact that we are no sooner in our good Master's presence than we immediately expand on our troubles and sins. This wearies our minds and weighs down our hearts with sorrow.... To avoid this danger, we should begin by expressing our joy: "Dear Lord, it's a pleasure for me to visit you. I'm happy to spend this short hour with you. How good of you to call me here! How good of you to love me as you do! From now on, I will love you intensely in return."

Then, in spirit, enter into the heart of Jesus to love and adore.

• • •

You wrote to me: "To pray is to talk with God. But about what?" About what? About him, and yourself: joys, sorrows, successes and failures, great ambitions, daily worries—even your weakness! And acts of thanksgiving and petitions—and love and reparation. In short, to get to know him and to get to know yourself—"to get acquainted."

—*St. Josemaría Escrivá de Balaguer*

• • •

Let your prayer be completely simple, for both the publican and the prodigal son were reconciled to God by a single phrase....

Let there be no studied elegance in the words of your prayers. How often the simple and monotonous lispings of little children make their fathers give in to them....

Do not launch out into long discussions that fritter away your mind in efforts for eloquence....A single word full of faith saved the good thief.

—*St. John Climacus*

• • •

However quietly we speak, he is so near that he will hear us: we need no wings to go in search of him but have only to find a place where we can be alone and look upon him present within us. Nor need we feel strange in the presence of so kind a Guest; we must talk to him very humbly, as we should to our father, asking him for things as we should ask a father, tell him our troubles, beg him to put them right, and yet realize that we are not worthy to be called his children.

—*St. Teresa of Avila*

. .

NO WORDS

For me, prayer is a surge of the heart, a simple glance toward heaven, a cry of gratitude and love in the midst of trial as well as joy.

—*St. Thérèse of Lisieux*

• • •

You have undoubtedly experienced in your own life a deep, legitimate affection for your father or mother, sister or brother, when nothing is said. At that moment a simple look or handshake says it all; the entire heart is moved. The best in oneself goes out to meet the best in another, who experiences this deep affection. Those moments and those very simple expressions of love between God and ourselves are the essence of prayer.

—*Père Jacques*

• • •

When you feel invited to remain in silence at our Lord's feet like Magdalene, just *looking at him with your heart*, without saying anything, don't cast about for any thoughts or reasonings, but just remain in loving adoration.

—*Bl. Columba Marmion*

• • •

During one time of prayer, Bl. Marie of the Incarnation found herself unable to express to God her great longing for him.

Thus I said to him: "You understand, O Love, you understand." Then words failed me completely and I remained in this silence.

CHAPTER FIVE

The Book That Comes Alive

If personal prayer is an opportunity for encountering God, it makes sense to go into it Bible in hand. No prayer book compares with God's Word, which not only inspires our listening and speaking to God but communicates his presence. As Vatican II put it: "In the sacred books the Father who is in heaven comes lovingly to meet his children, and talks with them…. Let them remember, however, that prayer should accompany the reading of sacred Scripture, so that a dialogue takes place between God and man" (*Dei Verbum* 21, 25).

The saints pursued this dialogue by praying with the Bible, especially the psalms and the Gospels. Some saints also dedicated themselves to Scripture study so as to make the whole Bible more accessible to others.

The great fourth-century scholar St. Jerome undertook to provide not just commentaries but an accurate Latin Bible. The massive project took twenty-two years, not counting time spent mastering Greek, Latin, and—"with much toil and effort"—even Hebrew. Driving his scholarly efforts was the conviction that "ignorance of the Scriptures is ignorance of Christ" and that Christians need guides who can show them "Jesus concealed beneath the letter."

St. Jerome came to Scripture study via a frightening dream in which he saw himself before the heavenly judgment seat.

"Whose disciple are you?" the Judge asked.

"Christ's," Jerome answered.

"You're lying," replied the Judge. "You're Cicero's disciple, not Christ's."

Afterward a shaken Jerome admitted that his addiction to the elegant writing of pagan authors like Cicero had left him unable to open the Bible without shuddering at what he considered its uncouth style. Deeply repentant, he threw himself into biblical studies, communicating his findings through personal instruction as well as writing, especially in the monastic communities he founded in Bethlehem. Some of his disciples, among them St. Paula and St. Marcella, themselves became knowledgeable guides to Scripture.

Any honest biography of St. Jerome reveals him as a perplexing mix of scholarship, piety, and irascibility. "Patron saint of grouches," a friend of mine calls him. At the same time, Jerome is admirable for his austerities, compassion for the poor, and zeal to meet Jesus in his Word.

Because my husband and I often write about the Bible, we have gotten into the habit of praying nightly to St. Jerome. As you reflect on the place of Scripture in your own life, you might want to invoke him too.

St. Jerome, pray for us.

APPROACHING THE BIBLE

Anyone who thirsts for God eagerly studies and meditates on the inspired word, knowing that there he is certain to find the one for whom he thirsts.

—*St. Bernard of Clairvaux*

A number of saints left prayers that we can use as we sit down to read Scripture. This one, which focuses on the Gospel accounts of Christ's suffering and death, is from St. Thomas More.

Good Lord, give us your grace not to read or hear this Gospel of your bitter Passion with our eyes and ears in the manner of a pastime. But may it, with compassion, so sink into our hearts that it may serve for the everlasting profit of our souls.

• • •

All sacred Scriptures should be read in the spirit in which they were written. In them, therefore, we should seek food for our souls rather than subtleties of speech.... Curiosity often hinders us in the reading of the Scriptures, for we try to examine and dispute over matters that we should pass over and accept in simplicity. If you desire to profit, read with humility, simplicity, and faith.

—*Thomas à Kempis*

• • •

Friends of St. Dominic left this description of how he interacted with God's Word.

He would sit quietly, and after the sign of the cross, begin to read.... His spirit would then be sweetly aroused as if he heard Our Lord speaking.... As if disputing with a companion he would first appear somewhat impatient in his thought and words. At the next moment he would become a quiet listener, then again seem to discuss and contend. He seemed almost to laugh and weep at the same time, and then, attentively and submissively, would murmur to himself and strike his breast....

Dominic used to venerate the book, bow to it, and kiss it. This was especially true if he was reading the Gospels and when he had been reading the very words which had come from the mouth of Christ.... Following this,...he would reverently rise and incline his head for a short time. Wholly refreshed and in great interior peace, he then returned to his book.

The Word That Speaks

Our meditations on the Word who is the Bridegroom, on his glory, his elegance, power, and majesty, become in a sense his way of speaking to us....When with eager minds we examine his rulings, the decrees from his own mouth; when we meditate on his law day and night, let us be assured that the Bridegroom is present, and that he speaks his message of happiness to us.

—*St. Bernard of Clairvaux*

• • •

Tested by illness and spiritual darkness, St. Thérèse of Lisieux was feeling "a bit sad" one evening toward the end of her life. Is God "really pleased with me"? she wondered, and she wished someone could tell her. Just then she was handed a note from her older sister, a Carmelite nun in the same convent.

"You told me that you were pleased with everything about me, that I was especially cherished by God," Thérèse told her sister later—but she was unconvinced: "Always the thought that your love made you see what wasn't there prevented me from rejoicing fully." It took a confirming word from Scripture to show Thérèse that her sister had spoken the truth.

I took my little book of the Gospels, asking God to comfort me, to answer me himself.... And it so happened that my glance fell on this passage that I had never noticed before: "He whom God has sent speaks the words of God, for he gives the Spirit without measure" (John 3:34).

Oh, then I cried tears of joy!… It's you, my little Mother, whom God has sent for me. You're the one who brought me up, who caused me to enter Carmel. All the great graces of my life I have received through you. You speak the same words as God, and I do believe now that God is very happy with me, since you tell me so.

• • •

St. Jerome gave this advice about Scripture reading to a young Roman woman named Eustochium in 384. Both she and her mother, Paula, are honored as saints.

Read often, learn all that you can. Let sleep overcome you, the book still in your hands; when your head falls, let it be on the sacred page…. Keep close to the footsteps of Christ, and, intent on his words, say, "Did not our hearts burn within us on the road while Jesus opened the Scriptures to us?" (Luke 24:32)…. Do you pray? You speak to the Bridegroom. Do you read? He speaks to you.

• • •

The farther I go into the Gospels and epistles, the more I find grace, strength, and incomparable life. God is indeed there. Every day I come away from this reading more satisfied and strengthened. My will is reinforced there, my heart warmed. Through this Book of books, God the Supreme Teacher educates my inmost being, helping me to understand life, to smile at duty, and to will more strongly.

—*Elisabeth Leseur*

PRAYING WITH SCRIPTURE

St. John Cassian's account of the advice given him by an Egyptian monk named Abba Isaac presents the spirit of lectio divina—*prayerful focusing on a Scripture text through reading, listening, and communing with God.*

To keep the thought of God always in your mind you must cling totally to this formula for piety: "Come to my help, O God. Lord, hurry to my rescue" (see Psalm 70:1).

[This verse]...bears all the feelings that human nature can experience. It can be adapted to every condition and deployed against every temptation. It carries a cry to God in the face of every danger. It piously confesses humility. It conveys our sense of frailty, our assurance of being heard, our confidence in help that is always and everywhere present. Someone forever calling out to his protector is very sure of his nearness.

This short verse is an indomitable wall for all those struggling against the onslaught of demons. Whatever the disgust, the anguish, or the gloom in our thoughts, it keeps us from despairing of our salvation since it reveals to us the One to whom we call, the One who sees our struggles and who is never far from those who pray to him.

If things go well for us in spirit, this verse is a warning. We must not get puffed up at being in a good condition that we cannot retain without the protection of God for whose continuous and speedy help it prays. This little verse, I am saying, proves to be necessary and useful to each one of us in all circumstances.

• • •

St. Teresa of Avila drew on her Gospel reading as an aid to personal prayer.

I would try to picture Christ as within me, [dwelling on] those times of his life when he was most lonely. It seemed to me that his being alone and afflicted, like a person in trouble, allowed me to approach him more easily. I had many simple thoughts of this kind. I used to find myself most at home during Christ's prayer in the Garden, where I would go to keep him company. I thought of the bloody sweat and of the affliction he endured there. Had it been possible, I would have liked to wipe that painful sweat from his face…. I used to remain with him there for as long as my thoughts allowed….

For many years, nearly every night before I fell asleep,…I used to think a little of this prayer in the Garden…. I believe that my soul gained very much in this way, because I began to practice prayer without knowing what it was.

• • •

Many Scripture verses make good prayers. Dorothy Day suggested using these three to ask for faith, hope, and charity:

Lord, I believe, help my unbelief (Mark 9:24).

In you I have hoped; let me never be put to shame (see Psalms 25:2; 31:14, 17).

Dear Lord, take away my "heart of stone" and give me a "heart of flesh," so I may learn to love, to grow in love (see Ezekiel 11:19).

• • •

A classic way to pray with Scripture: Put yourself in the place of various biblical figures—and not only the admirable ones!

I am the lost sheep and you are the Good Shepherd who hastened lovingly in search of me.... I am, alas! the prodigal son who wasted your substance, your natural and supernatural gifts, and reduced myself to the most miserable state because I had fled far from you....What more can I say? I am the treacherous disciple who betrayed you, the presumptuous man who disowned you, the coward who mocked and derided you, the cruel wretch who crowned you with thorns. I scourged you, I laid the cross upon you, I mocked you in your agony, I buffeted you, I gave you gall and vinegar to drink, and it was I, alas! who pierced your heart with the cruel lance. All this and even more I have done with my sins! What a thought to make me humble!

—*Bl. John XXIII*

THE BIBLE'S BOOK OF PRAYERS

Elizabeth Seton loved and prayed the psalms all her life. In 1803, as her husband, William, lay dying of tuberculosis while in quarantine at an Italian port, she kept their spirits up by reading the psalms aloud.

"Often when he hears me repeat the psalms of triumph in God," she wrote, "it so enlivens his spirit that he also makes them his own, and all our sorrows are turned into joy."

After William's death, Elizabeth experienced a "sad weariness" and hard soul-searching about whether to leave the Episcopal church: "So painful and sorrowful an impression is left on my heart, it is all clouded and troubled," she wrote a friend. "So I say the Penitential Psalms, if not with the spirit of the royal prophet [David], at least with his tears.... Yet with such confidence in God that it seems to me he was never so perfectly my Father and my All at any moment of my life before."

An exultant psalm—the first verse of Psalm 68—expressed Elizabeth's sense of joy at receiving her first Communion as a Catholic, when Jesus entered what she called "the poor little dwelling so all his own." She went on to say, "The first thought I remember was, 'Let God arise, let his enemies be scattered,' for it seemed to me my king had come to take his throne, and instead of the humble, tender welcome I had expected to give him, it was a triumph of joy and gladness that the deliverer had come."

• • •

If the psalm prays, you pray too. If it laments, do the same. If it gives thanks, rejoice along with it. If it speaks in the accents of fear, tremble with it. For all that is written in the psalms is meant to be a mirror for us.

—*St. Augustine*

• • •

Bl. Marie of the Incarnation experienced and recommended the psalms as "spiritual food" that "continually fills the soul with loving thoughts of God."

In the psalms I saw his justice, his judgments, his grandeur, his love, his equity, his beauties, his magnificence, his generosity.... I saw that the goodness of this divine spirit had established me in green and fertile pastures which kept my soul so nourished that it overflowed and I could not keep silent....

This took me so completely out of myself that as I went about the monastery I was in a constant state of ecstasy. It was the same while I was at work. Sometimes my thoughts were concentrated on the purity of God and how all things declare his glory. The psalm "the heavens declare the glory of God" (Psalm 19) had an attraction for me which pierced my heart and enraptured my spirit. "Yes, yes, O my Love! 'Your testimonies are true; they are justified of themselves. They give witness to the foolish' (Psalm 19:8). Send me over the whole world to teach those who are ignorant of you!"

• • •

I am easily cast down by suffering and would be inconsolable about my sickness if I did not find in the psalms those cries of sorrow...which God at last answers by granting pardon and peace. During many weeks of extreme fatigue, the psalms have never been out of my hands. I have not wearied of rereading those sublime lamentations, those flights of hope, those entreaties full of love which correspond to all the wants and miseries of human nature.... Though the psalms were composed long ago, we still find in them the expression of our deepest anguish and the consolation of our sorrows.

—Bl. Frederic Ozanam

TAKE AND READ

I'm always encouraging you—and I'm not going to stop encouraging you!—to keep on reading sacred Scripture. And don't let anyone say to me silly, contemptible words such as "I'm stuck at the courthouse all day." "I'm tied up with political affairs." "I'm in an apprenticeship program." "I've got a wife." "I'm raising kids." "I'm responsible for a household." "I'm a businessman. Reading the Bible isn't my thing."

What are you saying, man? It's not your business to pay attention to the Bible because you're distracted by thousands of concerns? Then Bible reading belongs *especially* to you. You're always standing in the line of battle, you're constantly being hit, so you need *more* medicine than other people. For not only does your wife irritate you, but your son annoys you, and a servant makes you lose your temper. An enemy schemes against you, a friend envies you, a neighbor insults you, a colleague trips you up. Often a lawsuit impends, poverty distresses, loss of possessions brings sorrow. At one moment success puffs you up; at another, failure deflates you. How many powerful inducements to anger and anxiety, to discouragement and grief, to vanity and loss of sense surround us on every side! A thousand missiles rain down from every direction. And so we constantly need the whole range of equipment supplied by Scripture.

—*St. John Chrysostom*

• • •

St. Ephrem's sheer delight on reading the book of Genesis holds out a promise of good things to come as we immerse ourselves in Scripture.

I read the opening of this book
and was filled with joy,
for its verses and lines
spread out their arms to welcome me;
the first rushed out and kissed me,
and led me on to its companion;
and when I reached that verse
wherein is written
the story of Paradise,
it lifted me up and transported me
from the bosom of the book
to the very bosom of Paradise....

Scripture brought me
to the gate of Paradise.

CHAPTER SIX

What to Do With Your Mind

Prayer is "nothing other than a raising of the mind to heavenly things," said St. Francis de Sales, quoting many earlier spiritual writers. "Yes, but you don't know my mind," some of us might retort.

"I try to pray, but my thoughts are all over the place."

"Most days, my mind is going a mile a minute. I feel too agitated for prayer."

"I'd pray better if I could just turn my mind off or make it blank."

If you've ever considered your mental processes a hindrance to holiness, you'll be interested in the saints' wisdom about how to make your mind an ally for prayer. Familiar with the same inner resistances we experience, the saints learned to use their thinking, willing, and imagining in turning to God. Some of them explored and explained the role of the mind in relation to various types of prayer—vocal, mental, contemplative. Outstanding among these spiritual guides is St. Francis de Sales.

Named bishop of Geneva in 1602, as the Catholic Church was struggling with the effects of the Reformation, Francis focused on renewing his diocese by leading people to deeper intimacy with God. Given his insistence that holiness is for everyone, along with his genius for teaching the ways of prayer, Francis is someone we can still seek advice from today. We can find it in his published letters of spiritual direction, in notes taken from his sermons and talks, and in his books. Read part 2 of his classic *Introduction to the Devout Life*, for example, and you'll come away with many insights into "what to do with your mind" when you go to pray.

As St. Francis points out, our minds themselves are changed as we bend them to prayer: "Since prayer places our intellect in the brilliance of God's light and exposes our will to the warmth of his heavenly love, nothing else so effectively purifies our intellect of ignorance and our will of depraved affections." Centuries before Francis, a saint named Paul touched on a similar point: "Do not be conformed to this world," he urged us, "but be transformed by the renewing of your mind" (Romans 12:2).

EVEN SAINTLY MINDS NEED HELP

Anyone whose mind has wandered at Mass will relate to St. Anthony Mary Claret's description of the distracted prayer he often experienced during his three years as a factory worker in Barcelona, Spain. A wise priest helped him out of his difficulty.

My only goal and all my anxieties were about manufacturing. I can't overstate it—my obsession approached delirium....

It is true that I loved to think and dwell on my projects, but during the Mass and my other devotions I did not want to and I tried to put them out of my mind. I told myself that I'd think about them later but that for the present I only wanted to think about what I was doing and pray. My efforts seemed useless, like trying to bring a swiftly rotating wheel to a sudden stop. I was tormented during Mass with new ideas, discoveries, etc. There seemed to be more machines in my head than saints on the altar.

• • •

It happens that the soul will be in the greatest quiet and the intellect will be so distracted that it won't seem that the quiet is present in the intellect's house.... Perhaps it's only my intellect that's like this, and others' intellects are not.... Sometimes I want to die in that I cannot cure this wandering of the intellect.

—*St. Teresa of Avila*

• • •

Although our outward aspect is appropriate to prayer, for we kneel and appear to those who see us to be praying, in our thought we imagine something pleasant, graciously talk with friends, angrily abuse enemies, feast with guests, build houses for our relatives, plant trees, travel, trade... consenting to any thought that comes along.

—*St. Nilus of Sinai*

• • •

Bl. John XXIII wrote this in his journal on Friday, August 24, 1900:

That blessed rosary went rather badly again this evening. And yet, I am sure I do not do this on purpose; every now and then, as soon as I notice my thoughts are straying, I do try to concentrate.

• • •

My God, how far I am from acting according to what I know so well! I confess it: my heart goes after shadows. I love anything better than communion with you. I am ever eager to get away from you. Often I find it difficult even to say my prayers. There is hardly any amusement I would not rather take up than set myself to think of you. Give me grace, O my Father, to be utterly ashamed of my own reluctance! Rouse me from sloth and coldness, and make me desire you with my whole heart. Teach me to love meditation, sacred reading, and prayer. Teach me to love that which must engage my mind for all eternity.

—*Bl. John Henry Newman*

No Mindless Repetitions!

I do not say mental rather than vocal prayer: to be prayer at all, it must be with reflection. For although the lips may be very busy, I do not call that prayer in which we do not consider with whom we are speaking, nor what we are praying for, nor whom we are to pray.... Anyone who has the habit of speaking to his Majesty as he would to his slave, not noticing if he speaks poorly, but who says just what comes into his head or that he has learned by heart for repetition, to my mind does not pray. Please God, may no Christian act in this manner.

—*St. Teresa of Avila*

• • •

To mutter something with the lips is not praying if one's heart is not joined to it.

—*St. Francis de Sales*

COMING INTO GOD'S PRESENCE

The practice of the presence of God is an application of our mind to God, or a remembrance of God present, that can be brought about either by the imagination or the understanding.

—*Br. Lawrence of the Resurrection*

• • •

Since we're praying to the Creator of the universe, says St. Vincent de Paul, it's only reasonable to prepare by asking ourselves questions like these:

How are we going to behave? Before whom are we to appear? What are we going to say? What is the grace for which we ought to ask? It very often happens that carelessness and sloth intervene, or hurry and confusion of mind prevent reflection.... This is a fault that must be checked.

• • •

St. Francis de Sales suggests four ways of placing ourselves in God's presence before we pray. Don't try to use them all together, he counsels, but one at a time.

The *first* consists in an alert, attentive awareness of God's presence everywhere—that is, that God is in all things and all places and that there is nothing and nowhere in this world where he isn't truly present....

The *second* way is to reflect that God is present not only in the place where you are but very specially in your heart and in the center of your spirit, to which he gives life and vitality by his divine presence....

The *third* way is to think of our Savior, who in his human form sees from heaven all the people in the world—particularly Christians, who are his children, and even more especially those who are praying and whose actions and behavior he notices. This isn't just imagining.... As St. Stephen was being martyred, this is how he saw God (Acts 7:55)....

The *fourth* way consists in using our imagination to picture the Savior in his sacred humanity as if he were near us, just as we sometimes picture our friends present.

•   •   •

Prayer consists in turning the mind to God. Do you wish to know how to turn your mind toward God? Follow my words. When you pray gather up your whole self, enter with your Beloved into the chamber of your heart, and there remain alone with him, forgetting all exterior concerns; and so rise aloft with all your love and all your mind, your affections, your desires, and devotion.

And let not your mind wander away from your prayer, but rise again and again in the fervor of your piety until you enter into the place of the wonderful tabernacle, even the house of God. There your heart will be delighted at the sight of your Beloved, and you will taste and see how good the Lord is, and how great is his goodness.

—*St. Bonaventure*

JUST IMAGINE

St. Jane Frances de Chantal described three ways of praying and advised people to pursue whichever one attracted them most. Here is the first, which is a matter of using our imagination to explore a mystery—here, the Nativity:

We picture Jesus in the manger, between an ox and a donkey, in the arms of his holy mother and of great saint Joseph. We look on as his mother places him in the crib, then picks him up to nurse him—to nurse this Son who is her Creator and God.

But don't get fixated on trying to see all these things too specifically, wanting to imagine what this holy infant's eyes look like and how his mouth is shaped. The point is to portray the mystery very simply for ourselves…. This way of meditating is good for people whose minds are filled with worldly concerns. If their imaginations are fully engaged when they pray, all other thoughts will be put to flight.

•   •   •

Among the types of prayer proposed by St. Ignatius of Loyola is the "application of the senses." In spirit, with the imagination, the person praying applies each of the five senses successively to subjects such as scenes from Christ's life.

The *first point* is to see the persons in my imagination, contemplating and meditating in detail the circumstances surrounding them, and I will then draw some spiritual profit from this scene.

The *second point* is to hear what they are saying, or what they might say, and I will reflect…to draw some fruit from what I have heard.

The *third point* is to smell and taste in my imagination the infinite fragrance and sweetness of the Divinity, and of the soul, and of its virtues, and of all else, according to the character of the person I am contemplating. And I will reflect within myself to draw spiritual profit therefrom.

The *fourth point* is to use in imagination the sense of touch, for example, by embracing and kissing the place where the persons walk or sit, always endeavoring to draw some spiritual fruit from this.

•   •   •

Use your imagination to explore different aspects of your relationship to God.

After offering myself entirely to God, I began to live as if only God and I existed in the world. Sometimes I considered myself before him as a miserable criminal at his judge's feet, and at other times I regarded him in my heart as my Father, as my God.

—*Br. Lawrence of the Resurrection*

• • •

Let us imagine that within us is an extremely rich palace, built entirely of gold and precious stones.... Imagine, too, as is indeed so, that you have a part to play in order for the palace to be so beautiful.... Imagine, also, that in this palace dwells this mighty King who has been gracious enough to become your Father; and that he is seated upon an extremely valuable throne, which is your heart....

All of this imagining is necessary that we may truly understand that within us lies something incomparably more precious than what we see outside ourselves....

In my opinion, if I had understood as I do now that in this little palace of my soul dwells so great a King, I would not have left him alone so often.

—*St. Teresa of Avila*

THINGS TO THINK ABOUT

In addition to using our imaginations, we can pray "by using our ability to think and reflect," said St. Jane Frances de Chantal.

We can consider the virtues our Lord demonstrated during his life on earth—among others, his humility, patience, kindness, love of enemies. As we think about these things, our wills will be moved and touched by God, giving rise to strong stirrings of the heart. These should lead to some practical resolutions for daily life.

• • •

I wish that every now and then you would go fishing. How? In this way. The holy Passion of Jesus is a sea of sorrows, but it is also a sea of love. Ask the Lord to teach you to fish in this sea. Immerse yourself in it. No matter how deep you go, you will never reach the bottom.

—*St. Paul of the Cross*

• • •

Try meditating on each word of the Our Father, in the manner St. Ignatius of Loyola describes:

One may sit or kneel accordingly as one feels better disposed or finds greater devotion, but should keep the eyes closed or intent on one place, and not allow them to wander. Then the person should say the word *Father,* and continue to consider the word as long as meanings, comparisons, relish, and consolations connected with it are found. The same procedure should be continued with each word of the Our Father, or of any other prayer which one wishes to use in this manner....

If the person who is contemplating finds in one or two words matter which yields thought, relish, and consolation, he or she ought not to be concerned to move forward, even though the whole hour is consumed on what he finds.

BEYOND THINKING

Spiritual reading can provide good subject matter for meditation, said St. Claude de la Colombière, but don't get too attached to what you're reading.

If you find good in it, don't change. [But] remember that every time you are filled with exceptional feelings, either of thanksgiving, or the love of God, or of admiration for his kindnesses, or of desire to please him, or of contempt for the things of earth, or finally, of his presence, you should make them the subject of your prayers....

Enjoy, prolong, increase the desire that God gives you of doing something for him. Make that the subject of your prayer as often as you feel moved by these thoughts.

•   •   •

Always prepare your mind for prayer by choosing a subject for meditation.... When your heart is moved and feels drawn to speak to God, to love him and converse with him, consider quietly and with loving respect his divine Majesty's wishes in your regard; and then, instead of meditating, think only of obeying him....

Above all, no matter what dryness or temptation you may feel, never give up prayer nor shorten the time assigned to it.... Be faithful, then, and be assured that God lets himself be found by those who persevere.

—*Bl. Marie of the Incarnation*

•   •   •

Meditation is the mother of the love of God, and contemplation is the daughter of the love of God.... Contemplation is nothing other than taking delight in the goodness of him whom we have learned to know in meditation, and whom we have learned to love by means of this knowledge.

—*St. Francis de Sales*

CHAPTER SEVEN

Struggles and Snags

Next time you feel discouraged because your prayer is dry, difficult, and devoid of God's presence, think of St. Jane Frances de Chantal. She said her own prayer life was "ordinarily nothing but distraction and a little suffering."

"Little"? When pressed to describe that suffering, Jane used phrases like "spiritual nausea," "a confused turmoil of darkness and helplessness," "feelings of rebellion, doubts and every other sort of horror." This was no passing phase either. Writing toward the end of her life, this outwardly serene and cheerful woman confided that she had endured her trials "for forty-one years now."

Providentially, St. Jane had the best of spiritual directors to help her navigate this spiritual minefield—none other than St. Francis de Sales. She met him in 1604, two and a half years after her husband's death in a hunting accident. Overwhelmed with grief, Jane had refocused and had adopted a rule of life that gave all her time to prayer, works of mercy, and the care and teaching of her four children. When St. Francis became her confessor, it was the beginning of an extraordinarily fruitful friendship that led, in time, to their cofounding the Visitation Order.

Francis told Jane how to handle her temptations to faith. Treat them like bees, he advised. "Don't fear them, don't touch them, and they won't hurt you. Pass on and don't spend time with them. You can be absolutely convinced that all the temptations of hell can't possibly stain a soul that doesn't love them."

Jane learned fast and passed along similar advice in her own letters of spiritual direction. "Do you know that these fears and self-torturings about your past confessions are pure temptations of the devil?" she wrote to a struggling nun. "Make a firm stand and take no heed of them, dear daughter, for the devil is only trying in his malice to deceive you. Pay no attention to anything the tempter suggests. Throw yourself on the mercy of the divine Mercy."

Never completely delivered from her temptations and sense of spiritual dryness, St. Jane learned to bear with them out of love for God. We can judge the results from this assessment by St. Vincent de Paul, who knew Jane well: "I consider her one of the holiest souls I've ever met."

DISTRACTED?

Leave at the door of the place where you are going to converse with God all extraneous thoughts, saying, with St. Bernard, "O my thoughts, wait here. After prayer we shall speak about other matters."

—*St. Alphonsus Liguori*

• • •

Thomas of Celano recounts an occasion when St. Francis of Assisi took vigorous action against a particular source of distraction.

One Lent he had made a little vase.... One day, while he was devoutly saying the Divine Office, his eyes turned to look at the vessel, and he felt that the interior man was thereby impeded in its fervor. Sorrowful therefore that the voice of his heart had been interrupted in its speaking to the ears of God,...he said before the listening brothers, "Alas, what a worthless work that has such power over me that it can twist my mind to itself! I will sacrifice it to the Lord, whose sacrifice it has impeded." When he said these words, he took the little vase and threw it into the fire to be burned. "Let us be ashamed," he said, "to be caught up by worthless imaginings, for at the time of prayer we speak to the *great King*."

• • •

The very pains we take to prevent distractions often work upon us as a considerable distraction.... If you begin to reflect and to turn your eyes upon self in order to learn what sort of attitude you are maintaining as you gaze upon...[God], then it is no longer upon him that your gaze is fixed but upon your own conduct and upon yourself.

—*St. Jane Frances de Chantal*

• • •

Who would put up with the behavior of a friend who addressed him but then turned away to speak to another person when we were about to reply?... Yet God puts up with the hearts of so many of us who pray while thinking about different things.... So then, should we despair of the human race and say that everyone whose prayer has been interrupted by wandering thoughts is condemned? If we say this, my brethren, I do not know what hope remains for any of us. But since we do hope in God because his mercy is great, let us say to him, "To you, O Lord, I lift up my soul" (Psalm 86:4).

And how have I lifted it up?

As best I could, Lord, according to the strength you gave me to catch it when it fled away.

And I can imagine the Lord saying, "Yes, but...every time you stood before me, you had such-and-such vain and empty thoughts and have hardly offered me a single word of undistracted prayer."

Yet I would answer, "'But you, Lord, are good and forgiving' (Psalm 86:5).... It is only because I am sick that my thoughts wander away. Heal me, and I shall stand firm. Strengthen me, and my attention will be fixed. But until you do, put up with me. 'For you, O Lord, are good and forgiving.'"

—St. Augustine

• • •

Distractions can be a means of purification.

As regards prayer, it is not less profitable to us or less pleasing to God when it is full of distractions. On the contrary, it will perhaps be more useful to us than if we had much consolation in it, because there will be more labor—provided, however, that we are faithful in withdrawing from these distractions, and in refraining from dwelling on them voluntarily.

—St. Francis de Sales

• • •

The whole aim of one who is beginning to pray, and do not forget this, for it is very important, must be to work and resolve and dispose herself with the utmost diligence to conform her will with the will of God.... Very often the Lord wills that evil thoughts and aridities should persecute and afflict us, without our being able to rid ourselves of them, and sometimes he even allows the reptiles to bite us, so that we may know how to protect ourselves better in the future, and to prove whether we are truly sorry for having offended him.

Therefore, if you fall sometimes, you must not be discouraged, nor slacken your efforts to make progress, for God can extract good even from these falls…. Place all your confidence in the mercy of God, and not in yourselves, and you will see how his Majesty will…bring you into a land where these wild beasts will neither touch nor annoy you.

—*St. Teresa of Avila*

• • •

Oh, the great illusion…to imagine that one has little or much virtue, according as one has few or many distractions in prayer. I have known nuns who were raised to a high degree of contemplation, and who were distracted from the beginning right to the end of their prayer…. Even though you were ravished in ecstasy twenty-four times a day, even though I had twenty-four distractions in reciting a Hail Mary, if I were as humble and as mortified as you, I would not wish to exchange my involuntary distractions for your ecstasies devoid of merit. In a word, I do not recognize perfection where there is no mortification.

—*St. Claude de la Colombière*

PARCHED AND PRAYERLESS

There are people who want experiences of God's closeness in prayer as a means of gaining perfection…. Nevertheless he permits them to be dry and parched, powerless and blind to the extent that they don't even know what they're doing. Well then, let's look for our perfection in this darkness and obscurity, by humility, patience, and resignation…. Seek peace in the midst of your trial, calm your mind in the midst of your restlessness by seeing the will of God in these things and by bending to his good pleasure. This will prepare you to receive the peace you desire so strongly.... Practice faithfully the holy teaching of our father, St. Francis de Sales, to refuse nothing that God's providence presents for our perfection and to desire nothing that is not given us.

—*St. Jane Frances de Chantal*

• • •

St. Francis de Sales understood that many of us go through periods when prayer and meditation feel joyless and boring. Don't be the slightest bit upset! is his first bit of advice. Here is more:

Pray out loud from time to time, using a prayer that is especially dear to your heart. Tell the Lord how unhappy you are about your sorry state. Acknowledge your unworthiness. Beg him to help you. Kiss his picture, if you have one, and speak to him these words of Jacob: "I will not let you go, unless you bless me" (Genesis 32:26).... At other times, take a book and read it attentively until your spirit is awakened and renewed. Stir up your heart sometimes by some gesture or attitude of external devotion: prostrate yourself on the ground, cross your hands over your breast, venerate a crucifix....

If you receive no comfort after all this, don't worry, no matter how great your dryness. Just remain before your God in a devout attitude. How many courtiers enter the prince's chambers a hundred times a year with no hope of speaking to him, but just to be seen by him and to do their duty! This is how we should come to prayer...purely and simply to do our duty and show our fidelity.

• • •

Sometimes when I find myself spiritually in dryness so great that I cannot produce a single good thought, I recite very slowly an Our Father or a Hail Mary. These prayers alone console me. They nourish my soul.

—*St. Thérèse of Lisieux*

. . .

Whenever you go to pray, keep in mind that it is the Lord your God who has invited you and that he wants to give you all the help and grace you need to pray well. If you experience dryness and aridity,…it may be a trial sent from God. Bear it patiently. Remain humbly at his feet, and assure him that you want to do only what is pleasing to him.

At other times, this difficulty and heaviness of spirit may arise from your lack of preparation for prayer, your inattention, self-indulgence, or attachment to things that lead you away from God. In that case, you must act quickly, asking our Lord to give you strength to remove the obstacles that stand in the way of your perfect union with him in prayer….

Appeal to the Divine Physician of souls. Ask him to help you see your spiritual weaknesses and to give you the grace to remedy them. Have total confidence in God's mercy and goodness. In this way, you will be able to keep from becoming careless and lukewarm, and you will become closely united with him in fervent, focused meditation.

—*St. Mary Euphrasia Pelletier*

. . .

If the tediousness that assails is very great, divide your meditation into several parts, and employ yourself mainly in petitions to God…. It's enough to repeat, "My Jesus, mercy. Lord, have mercy on us."

—*St. Alphonsus Liguori*

· ❦ ·
Dark Nights

In meditation, prayer, Communion I find no soul. In that tabernacle I know he is, but I see it not, feel not. A thousand deaths might hang over me to compel me to deny his presence there, and I would embrace them all rather than deny it an instant. Yet it seems that he is not there for me.

—*St. Elizabeth Seton*

• • •

When people have been growing in virtue and persevering in prayer for a time, says St. John of the Cross, God leads them into deeper prayer by allowing them to undergo a "dark night of the soul," in which he seems very far away. They struggle to pray as they used to, "but this trouble that they are taking is quite useless," says St. John: "God is now leading them by another road, which is that of contemplation, and it is very different from the first."

It is well for those who find themselves in this condition to take comfort, to persevere in patience and to be in no wise afflicted. Let them trust in God, who abandons not those that seek him with a simple and right heart, and will not fail to give them what is needful for the road, until he bring them into the clear and pure light of love....

The way in which they are to conduct themselves in this night of sense is to devote themselves not at all to reasoning and meditation, since this is not the time for it, but to allow the soul to remain in peace and quietness, although it may seem clear to them that they are doing nothing and are wasting their time, and although it may appear to them that it is because of their weakness that they have no desire in that state to think of anything. The truth is that they will be doing quite sufficient if they have patience and persevere in prayer without making any effort.

• • •

I thank my Jesus for making me walk in darkness. In it I am wrapped in profound peace.

—*St. Thérèse of Lisieux*

• • •

Therefore during this time of suffering and desolation I say to God: My Lord, let the world and even the devil take for themselves what I cannot prevent them having, but they shall never have anything to do with my heart, my will that you have left in my possession—this belongs to you; take it, it is yours, and do what you will with it."

—*St. Claude de la Colombière*

• • •

Bl. Teresa of Calcutta lived so joyfully and smiled so radiantly that no one could tell she was experiencing inner anguish. Not until ten years after her death, when a collection of her letters and personal writings was published in 2007, did it emerge that she had spent the last decades of her life in almost total spiritual darkness. This is from a letter to her confessor in 1959:

They think my faith, trust & love are filling my very being & that the intimacy with God and union to his will must be absorbing my heart.— Could they but know—and how my cheerfulness is the cloak by which I cover my emptiness and misery.

In spite of all—this darkness & emptiness is not as painful as the longing for God….What are you doing, my God, to one so small? When you asked to imprint your Passion on my heart—is this the answer?

If this brings you glory…if souls are brought to you…here I am, Lord, with joy I accept all to the end of life—& I will smile at your hidden face—always.

Never abandon prayer because you think you are no good at it. Do not be astonished, those of you who are newcomers, to see a month, two months, three months, six months pass by without any advance. No, not even a year or two years or three! And do not cease to go to prayer as if you were making a great advance in it. St. Teresa was twenty years without being able to pray.... And at the end of twenty years, God rewarded her perseverance.... How do you know...but that God wishes to make St. Teresas of you? How do you know what reward he may wish to bestow on your perseverance?...

Ask God to give you the grace of prayer,...ask him ceaselessly. It is an alms that you beg of him. It is not possible, if you persevere, for him to refuse you.

—*St. Vincent de Paul*

CHAPTER EIGHT

Try This

When you love someone, you're always on the lookout for ways to express your affection—thoughtful gifts, tender words, acts of kindness, attentive listening. The saints are people who related to God like this in their prayer life. Watching them at prayer, we see loving creativity at work.

A late thirteenth-century document gives us a privileged look at some of St. Dominic's ways of praying. Written by an anonymous author, it was based on eyewitness information from men and women in the religious communities Dominic founded. Since body language was an important aspect of his prayer, early manuscripts of "The Nine Ways of Prayer of St. Dominic" included miniature drawings illustrating his various prayer postures. Here are six of the "nine ways."

First Way: Dominic, "standing erect, bowed his head and humbly considering Christ, his Head, compared his lowliness with the excellence of Christ." Aloud, he offered prayers like, "Lord, I am not worthy to have you come under my roof" (Matthew 8:8).

Second Way: He also prayed "by throwing himself outstretched upon the ground, lying on his face." St. Dominic wept for his own and others' sins, using words like "God, be merciful to me, a sinner'" (Luke 18:13).

Fourth Way: Dominic liked to stand before a crucifix and look at it "with perfect attention" and frequent genuflections.

Fifth Way: "Often his hands would be extended before his breast in the manner of an open book," as if he were reading in God's presence. "He would sometimes join his hands, clasping them firmly together.... At other times he would raise his hands to his shoulders as the priest does at Mass."

Sixth Way: St. Dominic sometimes prayed standing, "with his hands and arms outstretched forcefully in the form of a cross."

Seventh Way: Often he reached up, "like an arrow which has been shot from a taut bow straight upwards into the sky." Sometimes his upraised hands were joined; other times, "slightly separated as if about to receive something from heaven."

By example and instruction, St. Dominic "constantly taught the friars to pray in this way," urging them on with psalm verses such as "Come, bless the Lord, all you servants of the Lord!... Lift up your hands, ...and bless the Lord" (Psalm 134:1, 2).

WINGS OF PRAYER

If you want your prayers to fly to God, equip them with the two wings of fasting and almsgiving.

—*St. Augustine*

• • •

Fasting gives us devotion and confidence at prayer. And notice how prayer and fasting assist each other like two allies, according to what is written: "When a brother helps a brother, both shall be comforted" (Proverbs 18:19). Prayer obtains the strength for fasting, and fasting merits the grace to pray. Fasting renders prayer more powerful, and prayer responds by sanctifying the fast and presenting it to the Lord.

—*St. Bernard of Clairvaux*

• • •

St. Angela Merici instructed her followers to fast.

For Scripture says, "Prayer is good with fasting" (see Tobit 12:8). And in the Bible we read, "Anna, daughter of Phanuel, who day and night served God in the Temple with fasting and prayer" (Luke 2:37). And as by fasting we mortify the carnal appetites and the senses, so by prayer we beg God for the true grace of spiritual life.

• • •

He who wishes to pray without mortifying himself is like a bird trying to fly before it has feathers.

—*St. Philip Neri*

• • •

Prayer knocks at the door, fasting obtains, mercy receives. Prayer, mercy, and fasting: these three are one and they give life to each other.

Fasting is the soul of prayer, mercy is the lifeblood of fasting. Let no one try to separate them, they cannot be separated. If you have only one of them or not all together, you have nothing. So if you pray, fast; if you fast, show mercy; if you want your petition to be heard, hear the petition of others. If you do not close your ear to others you open God's ear to yourself.

—*St. Peter Chrysologus*

PICTURE THIS

Looking for a prayer partner? Picture Jesus beside you, says St. Teresa of Avila.

Imagine that this Lord himself is at your side and see how lovingly and how humbly he is teaching you—and believe me, you should stay with so good a Friend for as long as you can before you leave him. If you become accustomed to having him at your side, and if he sees that you love him to be there and are always trying to please him, you will never be able, as we put it, to send him away, nor will he ever fail you. He will help you in all your trials and you will have him everywhere. Do you think it is a small thing to have such a Friend as that beside you?

• • •

Imagine Christ our Lord before you, hanging upon the cross. Speak with him of how, being the Creator he then became man and how, possessing eternal life, he submitted to temporal death to die for our sins.

Then I shall meditate upon myself and ask, "What have I done for Christ? What am I now doing for Christ?" As I see him in this condition, hanging upon the cross, I shall meditate on the thoughts that come to my mind.

—*St. Ignatius of Loyola*

• • •

Growing up, St. Anthony Mary Claret loved to pray in church before an image of Our Lady of the Rosary.

I talked and prayed so trustingly that I was quite sure the Blessed Virgin heard me. I used to imagine a sort of wire running from the image in front of me to its heavenly original. Although I had not yet seen a telegraph line at that time, I had imagined how it would be to have a telegraph line to heaven.

• • •

Some of the young women who joined the Sisters of Charity were illiterate and thought this might be an obstacle to meditation. Not at all, St. Vincent de Paul told them. Until they learned to read the Gospels, they could use visual aids.

Have in your hands pictures of the mysteries you intend to meditate on. While looking at them, you may think, "What is that? What's the meaning of that?" And so your mind will be opened.

A servant of God used to pray in this way. Looking at a picture of the Blessed Virgin, she considered the eyes, and said: "What use did you make of your eyes, O Blessed Mother?" And an interior voice replied: …. "I took great pleasure in beholding my Son; and while looking at him I was raised to the love of God."

• • •

Anyone can pray like this, said St. Vincent. "All you need is an image or a picture. Our Lord will surely say something to you."

• • •

St. Teresa of Avila liked to meditate on holy images and recommended the practice to others: "Try to carry about an image or painting of this Lord that is to your liking, not so as to carry it about on your heart and never look at it but so as to speak often with him; for he will inspire you with what to say." She herself returned again and again to Jesus' conversation with the woman at the well (see John 4:4–42).

Oh, how many times have I remembered the living water that the Lord told the Samaritan woman about! I have always been very fond of that gospel passage. From the time I was a little girl, without understanding this good as I do now, I often begged the Lord to give me that living water, long before I understood how good the water is. I kept a picture with me of the Lord coming to that well, with these words inscribed beneath it: *Domine, da mihi aquam....* "Lord, give me water."

CREATIVE EXPRESSIONS

St. Philip Neri had some prayers set to music. Many other saints— including those who belonged to religious communities that chant the psalms—sang their prayers. Ven. Solanus Casey, a Franciscan, was one of these. But he also had a more unusual way of making a joyful noise. Each Sunday evening for about a half hour, Solanus took his fiddle to the chapel and played hymns before the Blessed Sacrament.

• • •

Speaking of himself in the third person, St. Ignatius of Loyola describes the journal he started writing immediately after his conversion—an aid for meditating on ideas that had struck him in his spiritual reading.

He greatly enjoyed his books and the idea struck him to copy down, in abridged form, the more important items in the life of Christ and of the saints.... He set about writing these things in a book, taking great care and using red ink for Christ's words and blue for those of our Lady. He used polished and lined paper and wrote in a good hand since he had an attractive penmanship. He spent some of his time in writing and some in prayer.... The result of all this was that he felt within himself a strong impulse to serve our Lord.

• • •

I shall meditate as I have been accustomed, in the little Italian Church on Twelfth Street, by the side of the open window, looking out at the plants growing on the roof, the sweet corn, the boxes of herbs, the geraniums in bright bloom, and I shall rest happy in the presence of Christ on the altar, and then I shall come home and I shall write...and try to catch some of these things that happen to bring me nearer to God, to catch them and put them down on paper.

—*Dorothy Day*

• • •

You don't know what to say to Our Lord in prayer. Nothing comes to you and yet you would like to ask his advice about many things.

Look: take some notes during the day of the things you want to think about in the presence of God. And then go with those notes to pray.

—*St. Josemaría Escrivá de Balaguer*

• • •

Besides keeping prayer journals, many saints jotted down prayers or meditations. In this one, Bl. Frederic Ozanam expresses his thanks for the graces that usually go unnoticed.

We are not sufficiently grateful for God's little blessings. We thank him for having created and redeemed us and given us good parents and a wife and beloved children, and for giving himself to us so often in the sacrament of the altar. But besides these powerful graces,...how many more subtle ones are woven into the fabric of our lives!

There was the steady friend I met during my first year at college, who inspired rather than corrupted me; there was the older man who gave me a fatherly welcome and the woman who gave me good advice.... And even smaller things—an inspiration that prompted me to visit some poor people on a day when I was in a bad mood; seeing the appalling indignity of their situation, I went home ashamed at my imaginary woes. How often it happens that some inconvenience—say, a boring visitor I'd gladly wish away to Hong Kong—gives me an opportunity to do someone some good!

• • •

St. Philip Neri loved to say short prayers over and over, lingering over each word with great fervor. To better concentrate on the meaning of the Hail Mary, he condensed it into a single sentence— "Virgin Mary, Mother of God, pray to Jesus for me"—and made up a rosary consisting of sixty-three repetitions of this prayer. Another chaplet featured short prayers composed by Philip—simple, ardent statements to be said aloud, with feeling. Here are a few of those prayers, as handed down by one of his friends.

—My Jesus, don't trust me.

—My God, I wish to learn the road to heaven.

—What can I do, my Jesus, to please you?

—Holy Trinity, one God, have mercy on me.

—I seek you and do not find you. Come to me, my Jesus.

—I want to love you, my Jesus, but I don't know how.

—My Jesus, if you don't help me, I'm ruined.

—I distrust myself, but I trust in you, my Jesus.

VARIETY, THE SPICE OF PRAYER

There is nothing laid down about our posture in prayer, provided the soul keeps its attention when present with God. We ourselves stand when we pray, after the example of the publican, "who stood a long way off" (Luke 18:13). We also bend the knee, in accordance with what we read in the Acts of the Apostles (see Acts 7:59, 20:36); and we pray sitting, as you see in the case of David (1 Chronicles 17:16).... And unless it were right to pray lying down the psalmist would not have said, "I will water my bed with my tears" (Psalm 7:7).

—*St. Augustine*

• • •

St. Gregory of Sinai recommended variety in the manner of saying the Jesus Prayer, "Jesus Christ, Son of God, have mercy on me, a sinner."

Some teach the saying of the prayer with the lips, others with and in the mind. In my opinion both are advisable. For at times the mind, left to itself, becomes wearied and too exhausted to say the prayer mentally; at other times the lips get tired of this work. Therefore both methods of prayer should be used—with the lips and with the mind.

...BUT KEEP YOUR FOCUS

Haphazard reading, constantly varied and as if lighted upon by chance, does not edify but makes the mind unstable; taken into the memory lightly, it goes out from it even more lightly. But you should concentrate on certain authors and let your mind grow accustomed to them.

—*William of St. Thierry*

• • •

We owe much to those who in what they wrote enlightened our understanding.... But the book which speaks to the understanding but also awakens the will to the love of God should be held in high esteem. Hardly ever should we allow it to leave our hands. It should be read with the mind in repose, doing violence to oneself to pay attention, and casting aside every other thought.

Do not go jumping about from one book to another, nor begin by reading the end. For as a philosopher said, we enjoy variety in what we read, but perseverance in reading is what brings us profit. You should always pick out certain passages from what you have read and fix them in your mind.... Always have a definite time each day for reading, just as you should have for prayer and contemplation.

—*St. Alphonsus de Orozco*

• • •

It's good to come away from prayer with a practical resolution for the day, agrees St. John Gabriel Perboyre. Just don't bite off more than you can chew.

Be certain that if you make two resolutions you make one too many; and that if you make a new one every day, the end of the year will find you with all your faults and with nothing to offer our Lord but a mountain of infidelities. If St. Francis de Sales and St. Vincent de Paul had made new resolutions each morning, St. Francis would never have acquired the gentleness that won every heart, nor would St. Vincent have become a model of humility. It is important, you see, always to make the same resolution until we have perfectly overcome the fault we are combating or have acquired the virtue we desire.... Every day we should renew our resolution in our morning prayers, that it may be kept fresh and vigorous.

• • •

People who try every dish at a banquet, eating a little of each, disorder their stomachs so much that they can't sleep…. So it is with people who wish to try every method and means that might lead them to perfection….A certain discomfort and indigestion follows. This deprives them of peace and serenity of mind in our Lord's presence—the "one thing needed" which Mary chose, and "which will not be taken away from her" (Luke 10:42).

—*St. Francis de Sales*

CHAPTER NINE

Prayer's Best Teacher

"I am the mortal enemy of what is called 'direction,'" one of the twentieth century's most skilled spiritual directors wrote a friend in 1906. "The Holy Ghost alone can form souls."

Bl. Columba Marmion, an Irish-born monk and future abbot of the Benedictine Abbey of Maredsous in Belgium, wasn't trying to shock or to depreciate the help that comes from wise spiritual counselors. He was merely making the point that growth in prayer is mainly God's work.

Other saints said the same. "Don't suppose that prayer is a work of the human mind," said Francis de Sales. "It's a special gift of the Holy Spirit." And to a woman who wanted a method for mental prayer, Philip Neri said, "Be humble and obedient and the Holy Spirit will teach you."

Abbot Marmion himself was a student in this school of prayer. "I have a great desire to be guided, led, moved by the Spirit of Jesus in all things," he wrote. One reason for his eagerness is that he had already experienced the Spirit's transforming power. As a student walking into a study hall one ordinary day, the young Marmion had received a sudden "light" on the infinity of God. It was a pivotal instant that shaped his relationship with God for the rest of his life.

In books such as his classic *Christ the Life of the Soul*, Abbot Marmion insisted on the need not just to imitate Christ but to be transformed in Christ. This is a job for the Holy Spirit, he stressed, and obviously beyond human doing: "St. Paul tells us quite plainly that we cannot even pronounce the name of Jesus without the Holy Spirit (1 Corinthians 12:3). With much greater reason, we are incapable, without the help of this Divine Artist, of reproducing in our souls the features of the heavenly Model."

Columba Marmion's advice to us: See your prayer life as the Spirit's work from start to finish. Learn to recognize his voice. Follow his inspirations. Pray constantly to receive him.

> You may perhaps say: Have we not already received the Holy Spirit at Baptism, and yet more specially in the sacrament of Confirmation? Assuredly we have, but we can always receive him more abundantly. We can always receive from him clearer light, greater strength. He can always make deeper well-springs of consolation rise up in our souls, and enkindle within our hearts a more intense love.

THE SPIRIT OF LOVE TEACHES US

The Holy Spirit is the master of prayer. It is not surprising that God has given us this master to teach us the difficult lessons of prayer, since prayer is a supernatural work of love. There is no prayer which is not a work of love.

—*Père Jacques*

• • •

During Pentecost Mass in 1623, St. Louise de Marillac experienced an outpouring of grace that ended a period of spiritual anguish and made her vividly aware of the Spirit's power and action. From then on, says biographer Jean Calvet, she was a "disciple of the Holy Spirit" and turned to him "as towards that love which would make her worthy of the Father by making her more like the Son." Said Louise: The Holy Spirit "fills us with pure love of God....The Spirit makes us obedient to God, so that we may share the divine life."

St. Louise marked this anniversary for the rest of her life with a yearly Ascension-to-Pentecost retreat. Some of us may want to follow her example by using the same ten days in prayerful preparation for welcoming the Spirit of love more completely.

• • •

It is this Holy Spirit which will light in our hearts the flame of love.... How many know this Spirit of Love? And yet he alone is the source of their whole interior life.

—*Bl. Columba Marmion*

• • •

The Holy Spirit is the teacher of prayer. He enables us to live in perfect peace and constant joy, which is a foretaste of paradise.

—*St. Philip Neri*

• • •

I think that for certain people, our blessed Master takes on the task of doing everything himself. Real spiritual direction is a precious thing, but it is very rare. One can be comforted, upheld, and guided by a holy priest, but without finding the fullness of the guidance that our Lord sometimes reserves for himself. There are depths of soul which he alone can penetrate. He alone knows us fully, with all our unknown weaknesses, hopes, and misunderstood needs.

What we should ask from our spiritual director—in all humility, simplicity, and obedience—is a bit more light on our troubles, advice for our overall approach to our spiritual life, comfort in times of discouragement or suffering. But only in the heart of Jesus do we find the definitive support, deep strength, and total understanding of our soul and its needs that enables us to make progress and advance towards him.

—*Elisabeth Leseur*

• • •

The great method for mental prayer is simply this: that there is none when the Holy Spirit has taken charge of the person who is meditating, for then he does with the soul as it pleases him, and all rules and methods vanish away. In the hands of God the soul must become like clay in the hands of a potter...; or, if you like, the soul must become like soft wax receptive to the impression of a seal, or like a blank sheet upon which the Holy Spirit writes his divine will. If, when entering upon prayer, we could make ourselves a mere capacity for receiving the Spirit of God, this would suffice for all method. Prayer must be carried on by grace, and not by deliberate art.

—*St. Jane Frances de Chantal*

• • •

From a letter addressed to St. Francis Borgia:

For each one, that meditation is the best in which God communicates himself the most. For God knows and sees what is most suitable for us, and knowing all, he himself points out the way to be followed. But first we have to grope dimly, before finding this way, which will lead us to the life that has no end where we shall enjoy the most holy gifts of God.

—*St. Ignatius of Loyola*

God wants us to pray whenever we're in difficulty, said Bl. Charles de Foucauld, and in those moments the Spirit leads us to pray in one of two ways:

We can, like our Lord at Gethsemane, let nature speak and ask God to deliver us from suffering, danger or need, but in that case we must add immediately, as our Lord did, "nevertheless, let it be as you, not I, would have it" (Matthew 26:39). Or we could, silencing nature and letting only our faith and love of God speak, simply cry out, "Our Father in heaven, may your name be held holy" (Matthew 6:9), make anything happen as long as it is for your greatest glory. Do what you want with me, I only ask you for one thing, glorify your name to the utmost! Both prayers are good.... The Holy Spirit gives us an inclination toward one or the other; we only need to follow this inclination.

LISTEN TO HIS VOICE

Let us now consider what help to do good we receive from "the good Spirit" (Luke 11:13). He admonishes us, he moves us, he instructs us. He admonishes our memory (John 15:26), he moves our will, he instructs our reason.... He suggests what is good to the memory in holy meditations, and thus banishes from our minds cowardice and sloth.... As often as you become conscious of these promptings to good in your hearts, give glory to God and reverence the Holy Spirit whose voice is sounding in your ears.

—*St. Bernard of Clairvaux*

• • •

"In every soul, three spirits strive for mastery," Bl. Columba Marmion wrote in one of his letters of spiritual direction: the "spirit of falsehood and blasphemy," the "spirit of the world," and "the spirit of God." Train yourself to listen to the

right one, he advises.

I recommend you a great fidelity to the movements of the Holy Spirit. Your baptism and your confirmation have established him as a living fountain in your soul. Hear his whisperings, and put the other inspirations to flight at once. If you are faithful in this, little by little this divine Spirit will become your guide, and bear you with him into God's bosom. The Holy Spirit holds the place for us, that Jesus did for his apostles during his mortal life. Just as they could have recourse to him, speak to him, pray, etc., so he has sent us "another Paraclete to stay with us, and teach us all things which he has told us."

• • •

St. Frances Cabrini prayed constantly to the Holy Spirit and said that, of the mysteries of the rosary, the descent of the Holy Spirit was one she loved most. This exhortation, written during a sea journey from Genoa to New York in 1894, is typical:

Let us be faithful to the movements of the Holy Spirit...! Let our minds be pure, disinterested, humble, pliant, and then we shall see what beautiful and wonderful things the Holy Spirit will work in our souls.... This Spirit works within us, inspires us, instructs us, encourages us, and comforts us with his promptings and impulse.... From this we are able to understand that if we are not holy it is through our own fault.

• • •

If only we would receive God's inspirations to their fullest extent,...in no time we should be making great strides in holiness, heaven knows! However full a cistern is, it waters the garden only in proportion to the size of the pipes leading from it. The Holy Spirit, source of living water, embraces the heart of man to pour out his graces into it. However, he means us freely to consent to accept them, so he infuses them only as he pleases, and to the extent that we are disposed to cooperate with them....

This is the idea behind St. Paul's appeal: "We entreat you not to offer God's grace an ineffectual welcome" (2 Corinthians 6:1). If medicine were to be placed in a sick man's hand but he did not put it into his mouth,...it would do him no good. We too offer God's grace an ineffectual welcome if, when it is poured out in our hearts, we do not consent to it.

—*St. Francis de Sales*

• • •

What the Holy Spirit did for the apostles he will do for us.

—*St. André Bessette*

DEEPER INTO PRAYER

Wherever people are praying in the world, there the Holy Spirit is, the living breath of prayer.

The Holy Spirit is the gift that comes into our hearts together with prayer. In prayer he manifests himself first of all and above all as the gift that "helps us in our weakness." This is the magnificent thought developed by St. Paul in the Letter to the Romans when he writes: "For we do not know how to pray as we ought, but that very Spirit intercedes with sighs too deep for words" [Romans 8:26].

Therefore, the Holy Spirit not only enables us to pray, but guides us from within in prayer: He is present in our prayer and gives it a divine dimension. Thus, "God, who searches the heart, knows what is the mind of the Spirit, because the Spirit intercedes for the saints according to the will of God" [Romans 8:27]. Prayer, through the power of the Holy Spirit, becomes the ever more mature expression of the new human, who by means of this prayer, participates in the divine life.

—*Bl. John Paul II*

• • •

When we are faithful, every day, to consecrate a time, longer or shorter according to our aptitudes and duties of state, in speaking with the heavenly Father, in gathering up his inspirations and listening to what the Holy Spirit brings to mind, then the words of Christ…go on multiplying, inundating the soul with divine Light and opening out in it fountains of life….

Prayer then becomes a state, and the soul can find its God at will, even in the midst of many occupations….This state is more than the simple presence of God. It is an intimate intercourse, full of love, in which the soul speaks to God, sometimes with the lips, most often from the heart, and remains intimately united to him, despite the variety of the day's work and occupations. There are many souls, simple and upright, who faithful to the attractions of the Holy Spirit, reach this desirable state.

—*Bl. Columba Marmion*

• • •

Led by the Spirit, some people experience a kind of prayer that no human effort can produce.

God grants it to whom he pleases, when he pleases, and in the way he pleases. Man cannot teach it, nor can he attain to it by his own labor and effort. In this prayer the soul without any impulse of its own finds itself filled suddenly with light and holy love, and given understanding of certain truths which are incomprehensible to any other than itself.

—*St. Vincent de Paul*

. . .

Following an intense experience of God's love, Bl. Marie of the Incarnation found herself drawn into intimate conversation with God.

I was only twenty at this time, and my son was not yet a year old. My father asked me to come back and live at home; there it was easier to find some solitude. I lived on the top floor where, as I did some quiet needlework, my mind was occupied in its usual activity and my heart spoke constantly to God. I myself was astonished at the things my heart said; it spoke not at my prompting but was moved by a higher power.... It was absolutely incomprehensible to me that my heart should speak to him so intimately and so eloquently. But far from setting myself against it, I allowed myself to follow this attraction....

It must be acknowledged that the Spirit of God is a great teacher! Although I had never been instructed about mental prayer and mortification—I didn't even know these terms—he taught me everything, allowing me to experience the one and practice the other.... My heart poured out words of thanks, of praise of God,...of loving repentance, of pledges of fidelity in following whatever the Divine Goodness wanted of me.

. . .

St. Charles of Sezze describes the moment when the Spirit brought him into deeper, more heartfelt prayer:

Our Lord started showing me his mercy in this manner when one day I was praying before a painting of the Madonna in the church of the Jesuit Fathers in Sezze.... The image became so fixed in my heart and mind that I was completely inflamed with love....When I went to pray before the Madonna, I was changed into another person, losing thought and intellect in the divine light. Like one dazed I rested in my enjoyment and my soul was very content.

The change that came over me through this kind of prayer was very great. By the divine grace in it I was interiorly taught to do everything for God and I came to understand that without divine help our works are really nothing and have no value, even though performed with all possible exactness.

COME, HOLY SPIRIT!

I have prayed for you, that you too may be granted that great Spirit of fire, whom I have received. If you wish to receive him, so that he dwells in you, first offer physical labors and humility of heart and, lifting your thoughts to heaven day and night, seek this Spirit of fire with a righteous heart—and he will be given unto you.

—*St. Anthony the Great*

• • •

If you desire to correct your faults, and you feel that you cannot, if you languish with tepidity and it seems you can do no good,...try to be devout to the Holy Spirit, invoking him often and with your whole hearts. Stir up in yourselves strong desires to receive him, repeat often to him: "Create in me a clean heart, Lord, and put a new and right spirit within me. Do not cast me away from your presence, and do not take your holy Spirit from me" (Psalm 51:10–11). If you invoke him with a humble and trusting heart, he will descend with his blessed light and inflaming fire. He will come and penetrate into the very center of your heart, purifying it, changing it, enlightening it, inflaming it, and consuming it with the flames of his holy and divine love.

—*St. Frances Cabrini*

• • •

O you who are adorable, tremendous, blessed, give him to us! Send forth your Spirit, and we shall be made, and you will renew the face of the earth! (Psalm 103:30).

—*William of St. Thierry*

CHAPTER TEN

Pray Your Way Through the Day

Christians have always sought to "pray constantly"(1 Thessalonians 5:17)—that is, to find ways of keeping centered on God between times specifically given to prayer. If you've thought of this as an ideal that's incompatible with the demands of a busy life, you'll be interested in the saintly tips offered below.

Among Eastern Christians, the desire to "pray always" gave rise to the Jesus Prayer: "Lord Jesus Christ, Son of God, have mercy on me, a sinner." Modeled on the petitions of Gospel figures such as blind beggars and a desperate mother (see Matthew 9:27; 15:22), the Jesus Prayer is a trusting cry for help, constantly repeated at prayer and throughout the day. The seventh-century Palestinian hermit St. John Climacus said that this kind of prayer made present "the remembrance of Jesus ... with each breath." His fourteenth-century disciple St. Gregory of Sinai said that, prayed well, the Jesus Prayer leads to the highest forms of contemplation.

In the Western Church, many Christians have pursued continual prayer through "the practice of the presence of God." A little book by that name has become a spiritual classic. It was written by Br. Lawrence of the Resurrection, a seventeenth-century lay Carmelite who served as cook in a Paris monastery. Though not canonized, he had a saint's humble holiness and profoundly influenced the many people who sought him out.

As Br. Lawrence describes it, practicing the presence of God means offering him our "simple attention and general, loving gaze." It's "a conscious movement of our souls to God," recalling his constant presence and taking "great pleasure" in the fact. As we go about our daily business, "we can make our heart like a little chapel into which we retire from time to time to converse with God gently, humbly, and lovingly," said Br. Lawrence. "What can be more pleasing to God than to stop whatever we're doing a thousand times a day to worship him in our hearts?"

I like to picture Br. Lawrence in his bustling kitchen, where he said he experienced God "as tranquilly as if I were on my knees before the Blessed Sacrament.... I turn my little omelet in the pan for the love of God. When it is finished, if I have nothing to do, I prostrate myself on the ground, and adore my God, who gave me the grace to make it, after which I arise, more content than a king."

PREPARE TO MEET THE DAY

Most of us wouldn't come away from a walk in a beautiful garden without having picked a few flowers, observed St. Francis de Sales. Likewise, he said, before leaving our morning meditation, we should pick one or two inspiring thoughts and "remind ourselves of them during the day, breathing in their spiritual fragrance."

Along with this "spiritual bouquet," we should make some resolutions for pursuing virtue during the day. Get specific, St. Francis advised. "For example, if I have resolved to win over by gentleness the hearts of those who insult me, I will look this very day for an opportunity to greet these

people in a friendly way. If I cannot meet them, I will at least speak well
of them and pray to God for them."

. . .

Those words that struck you when you were praying: engrave them in
your memory and recite them slowly many times during the day.

—*St. Josemaría Escrivá de Balaguer*

. . .

The good thoughts which God gives you in prayer are relics. Gather
them carefully together in order to translate them into acts and you will
gladden the heart of God.

—*St. Vincent de Paul*

. . .

*One more counsel from St. Francis de Sales: Make a peaceful transition from
prayer to the day's activities.*

Keep silence for some time if you can, and move your heart very gently
from prayer to your occupations. Keep the feelings and good movements of the will produced in you for as long as possible....

You must get used to being able to pass from prayer to all kinds of
activities which your occupation and way of life require of you....The
lawyer must be able to pass from prayer to his work in court, the shop-
keeper to his business, the married woman to her duties in her family
and the bother of her household tasks, with so much gentleness and
peacefulness that their minds are not disturbed in any way. Prayer as well
as other duties are according to the will of God. So passing from one to
the other must be done in a spirit of humility and devotion.

A CHAPEL IN YOUR HEART

Bl. Raymond of Capua shares the secret of St. Catherine of Siena's unceasing attentiveness to God.

By an impulse of the Holy Spirit, [she] made for herself a secret cell within her own heart, and made up her mind never to go forth from it no matter what the business on which she was engaged.... [She] remained uninterruptedly within the walls of that inner cell of the heart which no one could take from her....

As I write this, old memories stir, and I bring back to mind how again and again she would recommend me when I was engrossed in all the work I had to do and crushed under the weight of it, or when I was about to set out on a journey: "Build yourself a cell within your heart, and never put a foot outside it." At the time I did not see the full implications of these words, but now I study them with a mind more ready to understand.

• • •

We can meditate everywhere—at home or elsewhere, even while walking or working....The person who seeks God will find him always and everywhere.The essential condition for conversing with God is solitude of the heart, without which prayer is worthless....

Deserts and caves are not essential to this solitude of the heart, which consists in being detached from worldly thoughts and desires. Even on the street, at resorts, and in public meetings, people who need to interact with the secular world can possess solitude of heart and continue united with God.

—*St. Alphonsus Liguori*

• • •

Writing to her married sister in 1905, Bl. Elizabeth of the Trinity shared a thought from St. John of the Cross: When we're at the deepest center of ourselves, we're in God.

Isn't that simple, isn't it consoling? Through everything, in the midst of your cares as a mother,…you can withdraw into this solitude to surrender yourself to the Holy Spirit so that he can transform you in God and imprint on your soul the image of the divine Beauty….

So the Father, bending over you lovingly, will see only the image of his Christ and say, "This is my beloved daughter, in whom I am well pleased" (Matthew 3:17)….

Every hour when you think of it…you can enter into the center of your soul where the Divine Guest dwells; you could think of those beautiful words…"Your body is the temple of the Holy Spirit who dwells within you"… and of those from the Master:"Remain in me, and I in you" [1 Corinthians 6:19; John 15:4].

THE DAYLONG CONVERSATION

God does not ask a great deal of us: a brief remembrance from time to time, a brief act of adoration, occasionally to ask him for his grace or offer him your sufferings, at other times to thank him for the graces he has given you and is giving you. In the midst of your work find consolation in him as often as possible. During your meals and conversations, occasionally lift up your heart to him….You need not shout out: he is closer to us than we may think….

Everyone is capable of these familiar conversations with God, some more, some less. Let's try. Perhaps he is only looking for the right intention on our part.

—*Br. Lawrence of the Resurrection*

St. Elizabeth Seton gave specific examples of how we might speak to God in various situations.

For instance, when you go to your studies,…look up to him with sweet complacency, and think: O Lord, how worthless is this knowledge, if it were not for the enlightening [of] my mind and improving it for your service; or for being more useful to my fellow-creatures, and enabled to fill the part your providence may give me.

When going into society or mixing with company, appeal to him who sees your heart…. "Dear Lord, you have placed me here…. Keep my heart from all that would separate me from you."

When you are excited to impatience, think for a moment how much more reason God has to be angry with you than you can have anger against any human being; and yet how constant is his patience and forbearance.

And in every disappointment, great or small, let your dear heart fly direct to him, your dear Savior, throwing yourself in his arms for refuge against every pain and sorrow. He never will leave you or forsake you.

• • •

Think about Christ's sufferings as you go about your day, said Bl. Henry Suso. And when you find your thoughts wandering, address him in disarming words like these:
Alas, my sweet Lord, what are you doing now? Where are you at this moment? Gentle Lord, come to me, sit by me, go with me and never leave me!

• • •

"What would Jesus do?" Long before people started wearing WWJD bracelets, St. Vincent de Paul was saying that asking Jesus' advice was an additional reason to talk with him all day.

Try to have constant communion with our Lord. Prayer is the source from which you can gain all the directions that you may need for your task. When any question arises, turn to God, and say to him: "Lord, you are the source of knowledge, show me what I ought to do in this matter."...

Be very careful to depend completely on the guidance of our Lord. I mean, when you must choose what you will do, ask yourself: "Does this agree with our Lord's teaching?" If you feel it does, hurry to do it; if not, you must decide against it. Whenever there is a possibility of undertaking good work, say to our Lord: "Lord, if you were here, what would you do? How would you teach these people? What kind of comfort would you give to these people who are sick or unhappy?"

PRAYER BREAKS

Go and find God when your patience and strength give out and you feel alone and helpless. Jesus is waiting for you in the chapel. Say to him, "You know, dear Jesus, what is going on....You are all I have.... Come and help me." And then go—and don't worry about how you're going to manage. It's enough that you have told God about it. He has a good memory.

—*St. Jeanne Jugan*

• • •

St. Teresa Benedicta of the Cross recommended a midday prayer break to seek God's help and perspective: "Then the rest of the day can take its course, under the same effort and strain, perhaps, but in peace." If at all possible, Edith visited Jesus in the Blessed Sacrament—a practice she had encountered at the cathedral in Cologne, Germany, before her conversion.

We went into the cathedral for a few moments, and as we stood there in respectful silence, a woman came in with her shopping basket and knelt down in one of the pews to say a short prayer. That was something completely new to me. In the synagogue, as in the Protestant churches I had visited, people only went in at the time of the service. But here was someone coming into the empty church in the middle of a day's work as if to talk with a friend. I have never been able to forget that.

• • •

Let's try not to perform any action without first offering it to God. And whatever we may be doing, let's not allow more than a quarter of an hour to pass without raising our heart to the Lord…. In our spare moments, too—when we're waiting for someone or walking in the garden or lying sick in bed—let's try to unite ourselves to God to the best of our ability.

—*St. Alphonsus Liguori*

• • •

How can I remember to raise my heart to God? Easy, said St. Vincent de Paul. Just use the sounds of the clock, and offer a short prayer whenever it strikes—or "beeps," he might say in our age of digital timepieces.

• • •

At night when you retire to rest, take your beads and go off to sleep while saying the rosary. Do the same as little children who fall asleep saying, "Mama, mama."

—*St. Bernadette*

· ❧ ·

P R A Y E R   C U E S   F R O M   D A I L Y   L I F E

Everything he saw pointed St. Anthony Mary Claret to God. Flowers brought to mind the virtues God calls us to seek. A tree loaded with fruit recalled Jesus' parable of the barren fig tree and inspired him with desire to produce the fruit of good works. When he heard birds singing, he thought of heaven's new song. Even the sight of a donkey inspired him to prayerful thoughts!

St. Anthony also found engaging ways of sharing his thoughts in conversations aimed at bringing other people to Christ. "I have personally witnessed the great value of conversations like these," he wrote. "Their effect was like that of the conversations Jesus held with the two travelers on the road to Emmaus [Luke 24:13–35]."

• • •

St. Frances Cabrini was afraid of the ocean. You'd never know it from the many sea-inspired meditations in her letters, which she wrote during her ocean crossings. Obedience to her missionary calling enabled St. Frances to find material for prayer even in something she feared by nature.

Blessed voice of obedience! When that speaks, the missionary crosses the ocean and gives no thought to the roaring waters and the rising and falling of the billows. Then the ocean becomes to her a sublime and magnificent sight that overwhelms her with admiration, fills her heart with God, and leads her to praise the Creator for the beauty and wonder of his works.

• • •

During a rough period when she was treated as the family Cinderella, St. Catherine of Siena lovingly carried out her menial tasks with the help of a mental image.

In her imagination, she said, she vividly pictured her father as representing our Lord and Savior Jesus Christ; her mother as his most glorious mother Mary; her brothers and the rest of the household as his apostles and disciples. Picturing them in this fashion she was able to render them a cheerful and unfailing service which filled them with astonishment....

As she went about her tasks, she kept her mind fixed on her Spouse, regarding herself as in reality serving him. Outwardly she was in the kitchen, inwardly in the Holy of Holies. Outwardly she was waiting at table; inwardly her soul was feasting on the presence of her Savior.

—*Bl. Raymond of Capua*

ARROW PRAYERS

Bl. Marie of the Incarnation urged everyone to speak constantly to God by sending up short prayers to heaven. She herself acquired the habit from her mother, Marie told her sister in a 1645 letter:

I remember when our departed mother was alone at her work, she used to take advantage of her free time to make short, fervent prayers. At such times, I would hear her speaking to Our Lord about her children and her troubles. Perhaps you didn't notice it as much as I did, but you would be surprised at the impression it made on me.

• • •

A brief lifting up of the heart is enough. A brief remembrance of God, an act of inner adoration—even though on the run with sword in hand—these prayers, short as they may be, are pleasing to God....There is nothing easier than to repeat these little inner adorations frequently throughout the day.

—*Br. Lawrence of the Resurrection*

• • •

A good way to train ourselves to pray these short prayers is to go through the petitions of the Our Father one after another, choosing a sentence for each day. For example, today you have chosen "Our Father who art in heaven." Start by saying, "My Father, you who are in heaven." Fifteen minutes later, say, "If you are my Father, when shall I be completely your daughter?" And so you will continue on to another part of your prayer at each quarter-hour.

—*St. Francis de Sales*

PRAY ALWAYS

We must pray literally without ceasing—without ceasing—in every occurrence and enjoyment of our lives. You know I mean that prayer of the heart...a habit of lifting up the heart to God, as in a constant communication with him.

—*St. Elizabeth Seton*

• • •

This encouragement to make the Jesus Prayer a part of oneself is from the Orthodox saint Gregory Palamas.

Let no one think, my brother Christians, that it is the duty only of priests and monks to pray without ceasing, and not of laypeople. No, no. It is the duty of all of us Christians to remain always in prayer....

Do not neglect the practice of this prayer.... This very name of our Lord Jesus Christ, constantly invoked by you, will help you to overcome all difficulties, and in the course of time you will become used to this practice and will taste how sweet is the name of the Lord. Then you will learn by experience that this practice is not impossible and not difficult but both possible and easy.

• • •

Whatever the object of my prayer,
I never pray or worship you in vain;
the very act of praying brings me rich reward.
Teach me then, Holy Spirit, to pray without ceasing,
that you may grant me to rejoice unceasingly in you.

—*William of St. Thierry*

CHAPTER ELEVEN

One Big Prayer Chain: The Communion of Saints

Dorothy Day was introduced to the communion of saints by a Catholic friend, "little Mary Harrington," when she was eight and growing up in a religiously indifferent family in Chicago. She "had told me of the saints and the Blessed Mother, and had so taken away all my fear of an awesome God and a vast and lonely heaven," Dorothy wrote of this discovery. Not for another twenty-two years would she be formally received into the Catholic Church. Still, the reality of the saints' friendship offered her hope, stirred her love, and developed into a distinguishing characteristic of her spiritual life as well as a support for her demanding work in the service of the needy through the Catholic Worker movement.

The saints became real to Dorothy—"new companions to look forward to meeting some day." Their life stories drew her to Christ and gave her examples to imitate. Their writings guided her into deeper prayer. Their intercession became a source of strength. Early on, Dorothy read St. Thérèse of Lisieux's promise that she would spend her heaven doing good on earth; that made her feel "even closer to all the saints," she said. She was especially drawn to Thérèse, Catherine of Siena, Teresa of Avila, Francis of Assisi, Joseph, and the Blessed Mother.

But membership in the communion of saints involves more than being on the receiving end of prayers from heaven. It means we ourselves intercede for the spiritual and material needs of other members of Christ's body on earth, as well as for those who are being purified in purgatory. Dorothy took this call seriously. Jim Forest, who worked with her at a hospitality house in a seedy section of Manhattan, reports: "One day, looking into the Bible and Missal she had left behind when summoned for a phone call, I found long lists of people, living and dead, whom she prayed for daily." In her *Catholic Worker* newspaper columns, Dorothy regularly invited readers to join her in praying for others, including deceased friends and acquaintances.

Dorothy Day isn't yet one of the Church's canonized saints. The process for her beatification and canonization was opened only in early 2000. But like the saints quoted in this chapter, Dorothy grasped the implications of belonging to a community that transcends time and even death and whose members are called to mutual love and assistance. Both in our prayer and in our pursuit of the works of mercy, Dorothy Day shows us how to do the same.

SAINTS READING SAINTS

It was a saying of St. Philip Neri that, both for study and for prayer, we should read chiefly "the authors whose names begin with S"—that is, the lives and writings of the saints.

• • •

St. Teresa of Avila read St. Augustine's Confessions *when she was emerging from years of "indulging in one pastime, one vanity, and one occasion of sin after another." She was drawn to Augustine, she said, partly because "he had been a sinner."*

I used to find a great deal of comfort in reading about the lives of saints who had been sinners before the Lord brought them back to himself. As he had forgiven them, I thought that he might do the same for me....

When I started to read the *Confessions*, I seemed to see myself in them and I began to commend myself often to that glorious saint. When I got as far as his conversion...it seemed exactly as if the Lord were speaking to me, or so my heart felt.

• • •

St. Teresa Benedicta of the Cross was searching when, in 1921, she came across St. Teresa of Avila's autobiography. Riveted, she read it all night straight through to the end. "This is the truth," she said as she finished the book. Then, over a period of time, she read St. Teresa's books aloud— "more as if she were praying them than reading them," observed one of Edith's Jewish friends. Edith was baptized into the Catholic Church on January 1, 1922.

• • •

I'm reading the life of St. Bernard...and it interests me very much. What a magnificent figure this monk is!... Despite our littleness, we can gain much through contact with people like this. They teach us to generously carry out the much more modest work that God asks of us in a simple, joyful, strong way—without looking at apparent results or at ourselves. Especially they teach us that suffering is the lot of Jesus' friends, that nothing great is accomplished without it, that it obtains all and digs the channel through which the great river of grace flows out to souls. Finally, the saints show us the infinite power of prayer and its hidden action.

—*Elisabeth Leseur*

• • •

When St. Ignatius of Loyola began reading the lives of the saints, he didn't have the slightest desire for high holiness. It was just that there were no other books in the house where he was convalescing from a leg injury. Speaking of himself in the third person, he describes how grace overtook him as he read:

While reading the life of our Lord and those of the saints he used to pause and meditate, reasoning with himself: "What if I were to do what St. Francis did, or to do what St. Dominic did?"... He used to say to himself: "St. Dominic did this, so I have to do it too. St. Francis did this, so I have to do it too."...

He began to think more seriously about his past life and how greatly he needed to do penance for it. It was at this time that the desire to imitate the saints came to him, and without giving any consideration to his present circumstances, he promised to do, with God's grace, what they had done.

• • •

Right now at our meetings [of the St. Vincent de Paul Society, which Ozanam founded], we're reading the life of St. Vincent de Paul...so that his example and traditions will sink more deeply into us. Indeed, a holy patron isn't a meaningless figurehead for an organization.... He's a model we must strive to take on for ourselves, just as he himself took on the divine model, Jesus Christ. We must continue this patron's life, warm our hearts in his, seek inspiration from his thinking.

—*Bl. Frederic Ozanam*

• • •

St. Anthony Mary Claret called St. Catherine of Siena "my teacher and my guide" and declared himself so moved by her biography that he always read it with "the book in one hand and a handkerchief in the other, to dry the tears it causes me." St. Teresa of Avila was another special guide: On two occasions, in 1864 and 1869, Anthony received deep insights as he read her works. No surprise that he chose St. Catherine and St. Teresa as copatrons of his Congregation of Missionaries.

SAINTS PRAYING TO SAINTS

For if it is lawful and profitable to invoke living saints to aid us, and to beseech them to assist us in prayers, as the prophet Baruch did— "And pray for us to the Lord our God" (Baruch 1:13)—and St. Paul— "Brethren, pray for us" (1 Thessalonians 5:25)—and as God himself commanded the friends of Job—…"Go to my servant Job…and my servant Job shall pray for you" (Job 42:8)—if then it is lawful to recommend ourselves to the living, how can it be unlawful to invoke the saints who in heaven enjoy God face to face? This is not derogatory to the honor due to God, but it is doubling it; for it is honoring the king not only in his person but in his servants.

—St. Alphonsus Liguori

• • •

St. Elizabeth Seton's children had heard Catholics pray the Hail Mary and wanted their mother to teach it to them. Elizabeth, still an Episcopalian, finally concluded: Why not?

And I ask my Savior why we should not say it. If any one is in heaven, his mother must be there. Are the angels, then, who are so often represented as being entrusted for us on earth, more compassionate or more exalted than she is? Oh! no, no, Mary our Mother, that cannot be! So I beseech her with the confidence and tenderness of her child to pity us and guide us to the true faith.... I kiss her picture...and beg her to be a mother to us.

• • •

St. Pio of Pietrelcina, better known as Padre Pio, had a special devotion to the Blessed Mother. He prayed the rosary almost constantly, as a way of meditating on Scripture and the profound mysteries of the faith.

May the virgin of sorrows obtain for us the grace to penetrate always further into the mystery of the cross. May she obtain for us the love of the cross, of suffering, and of sorrows, and may she who was the first to live the Gospel in all its perfection and all its seriousness gain for us the impulse to follow her immediately.

• • •

I took for my advocate and lord the glorious Saint Joseph and commended myself earnestly to him....

I wish I could persuade everyone to be devoted to this glorious saint, for I have great experience of the blessings which he can obtain from God. I have never known anyone to be truly devoted to him...who did not notably advance in virtue, for he gives very real help to souls who commend themselves to him....

I only beg, for the love of God, that anyone who does not believe me will put what I say to the test, and he will see by experience what great advantages come from his commending himself to this glorious patriarch and having devotion to him. Those who practice prayer should have a special affection for him always.... If anyone cannot find a master to teach him how to pray, let him take this glorious saint as his master and he will not go astray.

—*St. Teresa of Avila*

• • •

Long before he had any suspicion that he would become Pope John XXIII, Angelo Roncalli felt drawn to St. Francis de Sales for his gentle goodness. If only he could be like this saintly bishop of Geneva, he once wrote, he wouldn't even mind "if they were to make me pope!" The same journal entry, written in 1903 on January 29, the feast of St. Francis, ends with this heartfelt request to his heavenly patron:

O my loving saint, as I kneel before you at this moment, there is so much I could say to you! I love you tenderly and I will always remember you and look to you for help. O St. Francis, I can say no more; you can see into my heart, give me what I need to become like you.

• • •

Imagine yourselves to be spiritual beggars in the presence of God and his saints. You should go round from saint to saint, imploring an alms with the same earnestness with which the poor beg.

—*St. Philip Neri*

PRAYING FOR OTHERS

Prayer. In my opinion, this is the greatest means that can be used for the conversion of sinners, the perseverance of the just, and the relief of the souls in purgatory.

—*St. Anthony Mary Claret*

• • •

I rose at three in the morning...to pray for my neighbors in their needs....There passed before my mind's eye the different kinds of human suffering, men's weaknesses, sins, obstinacy, despair, sorrow, death, as well as the famines, the plagues, the other burdens they endure. Then there came to me the thought of Christ the Redeemer, Christ the Consoler, Christ the Lord God. I prayed to him by the power of all these titles of his that he deign to give help.

—*Bl. Peter Favre*

• • •

Beset by illness for much of her life, Elisabeth Leseur felt drawn to intercessory prayer—for souls in purgatory, the dying, priests, and especially for "God's conquest of the souls I love,…my husband, my mother, my dear nephews and niece, my sister, all the dear relations, and other people as well.…That is the object of my life."

Elisabeth loved the feasts of All Saints and All Souls—days when, as it seemed to her, the communion of saints made itself felt as a "more active, more tender" reality. She considered the communion of saints "one of the greatest joys of the spiritual life." One reason: "For those who, like myself, are almost useless to all outward appearances, it is very sweet to think that in God's hands, sufferings and sacrifices become active and beneficial, and that, passing through the heart of Jesus, they are transformed into graces for others."

Though she never flattered herself that her prayers had special power, Elisabeth knew they were effective: "I believe in them because I believe in that divine, mysterious law we call the communion of saints. I know that no cry, no desire, no call proceeding from the depths of our soul is lost; all go to God, and through him to those who moved us to pray. I know that only God performs the intimate transformation of a soul and that we can but point out to him those we love, saying, 'Lord, make them live.'"

Elisabeth had a premonition that her most cherished prayer—for the conversion of her husband, Felix—would be answered only after her death. This happened when Felix discovered her prayer journal and began a journey that led him into the Church and the priesthood.

• • •

I consider the loss of faith the greatest disaster and the greatest unhappiness.

How can one help grieving over friends and relatives and how insistent should be our prayers? We should be importunate as the friend trying to borrow some bread to feed his late guests, as the importunate widow before the unjust judge. But obedience to the command "Search the Scriptures" will give us the reassurance we need. Will a father, when he is asked for bread, give his son a stone?

—*Dorothy Day*

• • •

Only seven when Our Lady of Fatima appeared to her and two other children, Bl. Jacinta Marto was profoundly impressed by Mary's words about the seriousness of sin and by a vision of hell. The little girl decided to offer herself completely for the salvation of others. She prayed and took on many sacrifices—everything from giving away her snacks to enduring painful illness and a lonely hospital death just before her eleventh birthday.

"I'm so sorry for sinners! If only I could show them hell," Jacinta used to say. "I want all those people to go to heaven." And, "If only I could put into the heart of all, the fire that is burning within my own heart, and that makes me love the hearts of Jesus and Mary so much!"

Two powerful visions of a suffering pontiff drew Jacinta to special intercession for the pope. "Poor Holy Father, we must pray very much for him."

On May 13, 2000, when Pope John Paul II beatified Jacinta and her brother Francisco, he said: "I would like to celebrate the Lord's goodness to me when I was saved from death after being gravely wounded.... I also express my gratitude to Bl. Jacinta for the sacrifices and prayers offered for the Holy Father, whom she saw suffering greatly."

• • •

Almighty and tender Lord Jesus Christ,
I have asked you to be good to my friends,
and now I bring before you what I desire in my heart for my enemies....

You who are the true light, lighten their darkness;
you who are the whole truth, correct their errors;
you who are the true life, give life to their souls.
For you have said to your beloved disciple
that he who loves not remains dead.
So I pray, Lord, that you will give them love for you
and love for their neighbor....

I have prayed as a weak man and a sinner;
you who are mighty and merciful, hear my prayer.

—*St. Anselm*

• • •

Words of Our Lord to St. Catherine of Siena—and to us: Never cease offering me the incense of fragrant prayers for the salvation of souls, for I want to be merciful to the world. With your prayers and sweat and tears I will wash the face of my bride, holy Church.

CHAPTER TWELVE

It's All About Love

Rome, 1544. Alone in the catacombs, where he often keeps night vigils, a twenty-nine-year-old layman is praying earnestly to the Holy Spirit. Asking for the Spirit's gifts and graces has become a daily habit with him, but tonight, thoughts of the approaching feast of Pentecost stir him to special fervor. His prayer is answered in a sudden, unusual way: a globe of fire enters his mouth, setting his heart aflame with love. It is St. Philip Neri's personal Pentecost.

The effects of this encounter with God stayed with Philip for the rest of his long life. A large swelling formed over his heart, which from then on beat violently and radiated tremendous heat. (An autopsy after his death revealed an enlarged heart; over it, two broken ribs served as a protective arch.)

After this, Philip's whole life, which had been mainly solitary, became centered on leading others to encounter God's love for themselves. Literally burning with the fire of love, Philip often communicated it with a simple hug; on many occasions the sick or the sinful were healed as he pulled them to himself. Ordained a priest in 1551, he began an apostolate of the confessional, where his tenderness and gift of reading hearts led thousands to repentance.

He invited people over for informal sessions of prayer and discussion centered on Scripture. On these occasions Philip spoke from the heart, letting the Spirit guide his reflections on the biblical text. People came away stirred by God's love. Eventually Philip had a converting effect on the whole city of Rome—all because, in meeting him, people met Jesus.

Saints like Philip Neri reveal something of the ultimate effect of prayer, which is union with God through transformation in Christ. St. Paul pointed to the same reality: "It is no longer I who live, but Christ who lives in me" (Galatians 2:20).

Dynamic, radiant love that transforms us and overflows to others—if we pray, this is the goal toward which God moves us. Most of us will be struck by the discrepancy between ourselves and this chapter's descriptions of that love and its effects. Still, as we persevere and put our trust in God, he will do for us what he did for the saints. This story from the desert fathers—an apt commentary on Philip Neri's life—encourages us not to expect too little:

> Abbot Lot came to Abbot Joseph and said, Father, according to my strength I keep a modest rule of prayer and fasting and meditation and quiet, and according to my strength I purge my imagination: what more must I do? The old man, rising, held up his hands against the sky, and his fingers became like ten torches of fire, and he said, If you will, you shall be made wholly a flame.

The Delights of Loving God in Prayer

While I was about to go to Holy Communion, I seemed to be thrown wide open like a door flung open to welcome a close friend and then shut tight after his entry. So my heart was alone with him—alone with

God. It seems impossible to relate all the effects, feelings, leaping delight and festivity my soul experienced.

If I were to speak, for example, of all the happy and pleasant times shared with dear friends…, I would be saying nothing comparable to this joy. And if I were to add up all the occasions of rejoicing in the universe, I would be saying that all this amounts to little or nothing beside what, in an instant, my heart experiences in the presence of God. Or rather what God does to my heart, because all these other things flow from him and are his works.

Love makes the heart leap and dance. Love makes it exult and be festive. Love makes it sing and be silent as it pleases. Love grants it rest and enables it to act. Love possesses it and gives it everything. Loves takes it over completely and dwells in it. But I am unable to say more because if I wished to relate all the effects that my heart experiences in the act of going to Holy Communion and also at other times, I would never finish saying everything. It is sufficient to say that communion is a…mansion of love itself.

—*St. Veronica Giuliani*

• • •

To love Jesus is a wondrous thing…. There is nothing sweeter than love, nothing stronger, nothing higher, nothing wider, nothing more pleasant, nothing fuller or better in heaven or earth; for love is born of God, and only in God, above all that he has created, can it find rest.

A man in love treads on air; he runs for very joy. He is a free man; nothing can hold him back…. Love often knows no limits; its impetuous fire leaps across every boundary. Love feels no burden, makes light of every toil, strives for things beyond its strength….

Love is ever on the watch; it rests, but does not slumber, is wearied

but not spent.... Like a living flame, a blazing torch, it shoots upward....
A loud cry in the ears of God is that burning love for him in the soul
which says: "My God, my love, you are all mine and I am all yours."

—*Thomas à Kempis*

• • •

O infinite goodness of my God!... O Joy of the angels! When I consider
it, I wish I could wholly die of love! How true it is that you bear with
those who will not bear you! Oh, how good a friend you are, my Lord!
How you comfort and endure and also wait for us to become more like
you, and yet in the meantime you are so patient of the state we are in!
You take into account the occasions when we seek you, and when we
do penance for a moment, you forget our offenses against you.

I have seen this distinctly in my own case, and I cannot understand
why the whole world does not labor to draw near to you in this special friendship. Those of us who are wicked, who do not resemble you,
ought to do so in order that you may make them good. For that purpose,
they should allow you to remain with them at least for two hours daily,
even though they may not remain with you but, as I used to do, with
a thousand distractions and with worldly thoughts. In return,...you, O
Lord, defend them against the assaults of evil spirits, whose power you
restrain and even lessen daily, giving them the victory over these enemies. So it is, O Life of all lives, you slay none that put their trust in you
and seek your friendship; rather, you sustain their bodily life in greater
vigor and make their soul live.

—*St. Teresa of Avila*

• • •

Becoming What We Contemplate

It is through prayer that Jesus leads us to his Father. It is in prayer that the Holy Spirit transforms our lives. It is in prayer that we come to know God: to detect his presence in our souls, to hear his voice speaking through our consciences, and to treasure his gift to us of personal responsibility for our lives and for the world.

It is through prayer that we can *clearly focus our attention on the person of Jesus Christ* and see the total relevance of his teaching for our lives. We begin to see things his way.

—*Bl. John Paul II*

• • •

We cannot see Christ and remain as we are. We cannot exchange a look with Christ and not be overcome with a total conversion. If we are still tepid and still attached to our ease…it is because we have not exchanged glances with Christ; we have not really "seen" Christ.

—*Père Jacques*

• • •

Continual, humble prayer has a truly amazing outcome, says St. Catherine of Siena.

By such prayer the soul is united with God, following in the footsteps of Christ crucified, and through desire and affection and the union of love he makes of her another himself.

• • •

Prayer is the key to understanding and experiencing the depths of meaning suggested by Jesus' words in John 15:4.

"Abide in me": not for a few moments, a few passing hours, but abide permanently, habitually. Abide in me, pray in me, adore in me, love in me, suffer in me, work in me, act in me. Abide in me, whatever the person or action you are concerned with, penetrating ever deeper into this abode.... But to grasp the meaning of this mysterious appeal we must do more than listen to it superficially; we must immerse ourselves deeply, and more deeply still, into the Divinity by means of recollection.

"I follow after," exclaimed St. Paul (Philippians 3:12). So should we descend daily by this path into the abyss, which is God himself. Let us glide into its depths with loving confidence.... It is there that the abyss of our nothingness will find itself face to face with the abyss of the mercy, with the immensity of the All of God. There shall we find the strength to die to self and, losing all trace of self, we shall be transformed in love. "Blessed are they who die in the Lord" (Revelation 14:13).

—*Bl. Elizabeth of the Trinity*

• • •

Prayer unites the soul to God....

The whole reason why we pray is to be united into the vision and contemplation of him to whom we pray, wonderfully rejoicing with reverent fear, and with so much sweetness and light in him.... And well I know that the more the soul sees of God, the more she desires him by grace.

—*Julian of Norwich*

• • •

Place your mind before the mirror of eternity!
Place your soul in the brilliance of glory!
Place your heart in the figure of the divine substance!
And transform your whole being into the image
of the Godhead Itself through contemplation!
So that you too may feel what his friends feel
as they taste the hidden sweetness
which God himself has reserved
from the beginning for those who love him.

—*St. Clare of Assisi*

PRAY, LOVE, REACH OUT

Watch yourself to make sure there's a good fit between your praying and your living, warns St. John Vianney.

Night and morning you fold your hands and say in prayer, "My God I love you with my whole heart and above all things." And when praying like this, you believe that you are speaking the truth. And yet a few hours after, your hand may be busy injuring your neighbor; your mouth, which has expressed your love of God, will, perhaps, be soiled with oaths, tale-bearing, calumnies, and all sorts of slander, thus dishonoring and abusing that same God to whom you have just said that you love him with your whole heart. Do your actions prove your words?

• • •

Don't be thrown out of the heavenly banquet, says St. Augustine. Put on "the wedding garment of charity" that will let you in (see Matthew 22:1–14).

Extend your love, and not only as far as your husbands, wives and children. That degree of love is to be found even among cattle and sparrows....

But extend your love, let this love grow…. First love God. Extend your-selves toward God, and grab whom you can for God. An enemy, perhaps; have him snatched for God. A son, a wife, a slave, have them snatched off to God. A stranger perhaps; have him snatched off to God. Grab, grab your enemy; by being grabbed he will cease to be your enemy.

That's the way we should be making progress: that's the way charity should be nourished and eventually brought to perfection. That's how the wedding garment should be put on. That's how the image of God to which we were created should be progressively sculpted afresh.

• • •

When I see people very diligently trying to discover what type of prayer they are experiencing and so completely wrapped up in their prayers that they seem afraid to stir, or to indulge in a moment's thought, lest they should lose the slightest degree of the tenderness and devotion which they have been feeling, I realize how little they understand of the road to the attainment of union. They think that the whole thing consists in this. But no, sisters, no; what the Lord desires is works. If you see a sick woman to whom you can give some help, never be affected by the fear that your devotion will suffer, but take pity on her; if she is in pain, you should feel pain too; if necessary, fast so that she may have your food, not so much for her sake as because you know it to be your Lord's will. That is true union with his will.

—*St. Teresa of Avila*

• • •

My Jesus, penetrate me through and through so that I might be able to reflect you in my whole life…. Grant that I may have love, compassion and mercy for every soul without exception. O my Jesus, each of your saints reflects one of your virtues; I desire to reflect your compassionate heart, full of mercy…. Let your mercy, O Jesus, be impressed upon my heart and soul like a seal, and this will be my badge in this and the future life.

—St. Faustina Kowalska

• • •

When I began to taste God in prayer and in the reception of the most Blessed Sacrament, my heart was set on fire more intensely and I was moved with pity and compassion towards the poor. I was kind toward everyone and I tried to take care of everyone's needs without considering that thereby I would have to do without something myself. Our Lord joined faith and hope to my charity, and I firmly believed and trusted that he would be my sure provider.

—St. Charles of Sezze

• • •

We have been sent here not only to love God ourselves, but to make others love him. It is not enough for us to love God if our neighbor does not love him also….

If we have one spark of that sacred fire that glowed in the heart of Jesus Christ, can we remain with folded hands? Can we neglect those whom we might be helping? Not at all, because real charity cannot stand idle nor allow us to see our friends in need without showing them our love.

—St. Vincent de Paul

• • •

Prayer is powerful! It fills the earth with mercy....The mercy obtained through prayer will be like a torrent coming from that immense ocean of the inexhaustible goodness of the heart of Jesus. It will...quietly dispose people to approach God and enter into the ark of eternal salvation.

—*St. Frances Cabrini*

PRAYING FOR LOVE

O God, love, who have created me, recreate me in your love.

O love, who have redeemed me, whatever I have neglected of your love, amend for yourself and redeem in me.

O God, love, who with the blood of your Christ have ransomed me for yourself, sanctify me in your truth.

O God, love, who have adopted me as a daughter, nourish, nourish me after your own heart....

O God, love, who have cherished me gratuitously, grant that I may cherish you with all my heart, all my soul, all my strength, all my virtue.

O love, most almighty God, embolden me in your love.

O wisest love, grant that I may love you wisely....

O dearest love, grant that I may live for you alone.

—*St. Gertrude the Great*

• • •

Give me the grace, my Jesus, to love you out of love and not fear.

—*St. Philip Neri*

• • •

O you who have willed to be called charity, give me charity, that I may love you more than I love myself, not caring at all what I do with myself, so long as I am doing what is pleasing in your sight. Grant me, O Father—though I dare not always call myself your child—grant me at least to be your faithful little servant and the sheep of your pasture.

Speak to your servant's heart sometimes, O Lord, so that your consolations may give joy to my soul (Psalm 93:19). And teach me to speak to you often in prayer.

—*William of St. Thierry*

Saints' Biographies

St. Albert the Great (1206–1280). German; Dominican; philosopher, theologian, scientist; bishop; doctor of the Church.

St. Alphonsus de Orozco (1500–1591). Spanish; Augustinian; prior, preacher, spiritual writer.

St. Alphonsus Liguori (1696–1787). Italian; founder of Redemptorists; missionary, reformer, spiritual writer; bishop; doctor of the Church.

St. André Bessette (1845–1937). French Canadian; Holy Cross brother; healing ministry; founded Oratory of St. Joseph, Montreal.

St. Angela Merici (c. 1470–1540). Italian; founded Ursulines.

St. Anselm (1033–1109). Italian; monk, archbishop, political activist, theologian; doctor of the Church.

St. Anthony the Great (251–356). Egyptian; hermit, ascetic, a founder of monasticism.

St. Anthony Mary Claret (1807–1870). Spanish; founder of Claretians; writer, preacher, reformer, missionary; archbishop of Santiago, Cuba.

St. Augustine of Hippo (354–430). African; preacher, writer, theologian; bishop; father and doctor of the Church.

St. Bernadette Soubirous (1844–1879). French; received apparitions of Our Lady at Lourdes; Sister of Notre Dame of Nevers.

St. Bernard of Clairvaux (c. 1090–1153). French; Cistercian abbot; reformer, preacher, theologian, doctor of the Church.

St. Bonaventure (c. 1218–1274). Italian; Franciscan; theologian, philosopher, spiritual writer; doctor of the Church.

St. Catherine of Siena (1347–1380). Italian; evangelizer, political and spiritual advisor, servant of the poor, mystic; doctor of the Church.

Bl. Charles de Foucauld (1858–1916). French; priest, hermit, "little brother of Jesus"; his plan for prayer, witness, and service to the poor inspired five religious congregations; murdered in Algeria.

St. Charles of Sezze (1613–1670). Italian; Franciscan; mystic, spiritual counselor and writer.

St. Clare of Assisi (1193–1253). Italian; cofounder of the Poor Clares; abbess, mystic, influential counselor.

St. Claude de la Colombière (1642–1682). French; Jesuit; preacher, writer, spiritual director of St. Margaret Mary Alacoque.

Bl. Columba Marmion (1858–1923). Irish; Benedictine abbot, writer, spiritual director.

St. Dominic (1170–1221). Spanish; Scripture scholar and theologian; reformer, evangelizer, contemplative, founder of the Order of Friars Preachers (Dominicans).

Dorothy Day, Servant of God (1897–1980). American; peace and social-justice activist; writer; cofounder of the Catholic Worker movement.

St. Teresa Benedicta of the Cross (Edith Stein) (1891–1942). German; Jewish philosopher, educator, writer; Carmelite nun; killed at Auschwitz.

Elisabeth Leseur, Servant of God (1866–1914). French; wife, intercessor, contemplative, exemplar of redemptive suffering.

St. Elizabeth Ann Seton (1774–1821). American; wife, mother, widow; foundress of the Sisters of Charity; first U.S.-born saint to be canonized.

Bl. Elizabeth of the Trinity (1880–1906). French; Carmelite nun; mystic, spiritual writer.

St. Ephrem (c. 306–c. 373). Syrian; hermit; deacon; Scripture scholar, writer, poet, composer of hymns; doctor of the Church.

Evagrius (346–399). Egyptian; preacher, spiritual guide, one of the first desert fathers to write about the spiritual life.

St. Faustina Kowalska (1905–1938). Polish; Sister of Our Lady of Mercy; intercessor, visionary; inspired devotion to the Divine Mercy.

St. Frances Xavier Cabrini (1850–1917). Italian; founded Missionary Sisters of the Sacred Heart; served Italian immigrants in the United States; first canonized U.S. citizen.

St. Francis of Assisi (1181–1226). Italian; founder of Order of Friars Minor (Franciscans), Third Order; cofounder of Poor Clares; lover of poverty; missionary, mystic, stigmatist.

St. Francis de Sales (1567–1622). French; cofounder of the Order of the Visitation; missionary, spiritual writer; bishop; doctor of the Church.

Bl. Frederic Ozanam (1813–1853). French; husband, father; lawyer, scholar, writer; founder of the St. Vincent de Paul Society.

St. Gertrude the Great (1256–1302). German; Benedictine nun; Scripture scholar, writer, mystic, visionary.

Gilbert of Hoyland (d. 1172). Dutch; Cistercian abbot; preacher, writer.

St. Gregory Palamas (1296–1359). Greek; monk, archbishop, spiritual teacher and writer.

St. Gregory of Sinai (d. 1346). Cypriot; monk on Mounts Sinai, Athos; master and teacher of contemplative prayer, especially the Jesus Prayer.

Bl. Henry Suso (c. 1298–1366). Swiss; Dominican preacher, teacher, spiritual writer and director, mystic.

St. Ignatius of Loyola (1491–1556). Spanish; founder of the Society of Jesus (Jesuits); reformer, spiritual director, author of Spiritual Exercises.

St. Isaac of Syria (d. end of sixth century). Syrian; monk, bishop, writer.

Bl. Jacinta Marto (1910–1920). Portuguese; one of the three children to whom Our Lady appeared at Fatima.

St. Jane Frances de Chantal (1572–1641). French; wife, mother, widow; cofounder of the Order of the Visitation; spiritual director and writer.

St. Jeanne Jugan (1792–1879). French; main foundress of the Little Sisters of the Poor, providing special care for the elderly.

St. Jerome (c. 341–420). Born in Dalmatia; priest, hermit, monastery founder; translator and commentator of Scripture; doctor of the Church.

St. John of the Cross (1542–1591). Spanish; Carmelite priest and coworker of St. Teresa of Avila; poet, mystic, classic spiritual writer.

St. John Cassian (c. 360–c. 433). Romanian; priest, monk, monastic father and writer.

St. John Chrysostom (347–407). Greek; monk, priest, eloquent preacher; patriarch of Constantinople.

St. John Climacus (c. 579–c. 649). Palestinian; desert monk and hermit; abbot, influential author.

St. John Damascene (c. 675–c. 749). Greek; monk; theologian, composer; father of the Church.

St. John Gabriel Perboyre (1802–1840). French; Vincentian priest; missionary to China; martyr.

Bl. John Paul II (Karol Wojtyla) (1920–2005). Polish; pope from 1978 to 2005; global leader; influential thinker, writer, and communicator known for missionary outreach, travels, canonizations.

Bl. John Henry Newman (1801–1890). English; Anglican convert to Catholicism; scholar, teacher, writer, cardinal.

Bl. John XXIII (1881–1963). Italian; priest, Vatican diplomat, pope; convened Second Vatican Council in 1962.

St. John Vianney, the Curé of Ars (1786–1859). French; model parish priest and saintly confessor with a gift of physical and spiritual healing.

St. Josemaría Escrivá de Balaguer (1902–1975). Spanish; priest; founder of Opus Dei.

Julian of Norwich (c. 1342–c. 1423). English; recluse, mystic, spiritual writer.

Br. Lawrence of the Resurrection (c. 1605–1691). French; Carmelite brother; cook, gardener, contemplative, teacher of prayer.

St. Louise de Marillac (1591–1660). French; wife, mother, widow; cofounder of Sisters of Charity.

Lucien-Louis Bunel (Père Jacques), Servant of God (1900–1945). French; Carmelite priest, teacher; thrown into Mauthausen concentration camp for opposing the Nazis and sheltering three Jewish boys.

St. Macarius the Great (c. 300–390). Egyptian; hermit, desert father, founder of influential colony of monks.

Bl. Marie of the Incarnation (1599–1672). French; wife, mother, widow; Ursuline nun, mystic, missionary to Canada.

St. Mark the Ascetic (fourth century). Egyptian; desert father, spiritual director, writer.

St. Mary Euphrasia Pelletier (1796–1868). French; served the homeless and marginalized; founded Good Shepherd Sisters.

St. Nilus of Sinai (d. 450). Greek; monk, desert father, spiritual master and writer.

St. Paul of the Cross (1694–1775). Italian; founder of the Passionists; missionary, preacher, spiritual director.

St. Peter of Alcantara (1499–1562). Spanish; Franciscan; founder, reformer, spiritual director.

St. Peter Chrysologus (406–c. 450). Italian; preacher, reformer; archbishop; doctor of the Church.

St. Peter Julian Eymard (1811–1868). French priest; founded religious orders and organizations devoted to adoration of the Blessed Sacrament.

Bl. Peter Favre (1506-46). One of the first Jesuits; worked to heal the division between Catholics and Protestants following the Reformation.

St. Philip Neri (1515–1595). Italian; priest, founder of the Congregation of the Oratory; mystic and evangelizer.

St. Pio of Pietrelcina (1887–1968). Italian; Capuchin Franciscan priest; stigmatist, intercessor, confessor; supernatural gifts of bilocation, prophecy, visions, and healing.

Bl. Raymond of Capua (1333–1399). Italian; Dominican priest; spiritual director and biographer of St. Catherine of Siena.

Ven. Solanus Casey (1870–1957). American; Capuchin Franciscan; porter, spiritual counselor with a healing ministry.

Bl. Teresa of Calcutta (1910–1997). Albanian; Sister of Loreto; founded the Missionaries of Charity serving the "poorest of the poor"; global figure of joyful simplicity, sacrifice.

St. Teresa of Avila (1515–1582). Spanish; Carmelite nun; reformer, writer, teacher of prayer; doctor of the Church.

St. Thérèse of Lisieux (1873–1897). French; Carmelite nun; teacher of prayer; doctor of the Church.

Thomas à Kempis (c. 1379–1471). Dutch; Augustinian canon; preacher, spiritual director; wrote *The Imitation of Christ.*

St. Thomas Aquinas (1225–1274). Italian; Dominican theologian, philosopher, teacher, writer; doctor of the Church.

St. Thomas More (1477–1535). English; husband, father; scholar, humanist, chancellor of England; beheaded for refusing to acknowledge King Henry VIII as head of the Church in England.

Bl. Titus Brandsma (1881–1942). Dutch; Carmelite priest; philosophy professor, writer, friend to the poor; killed at Dachau.

St. Veronica Giuliani (1660–1727). Italian; Capuchin abbess; spiritual writer, mystic, stigmatist, visionary.

St. Vincent de Paul (1581–1660). French; founder of many outreaches to the poor, sick, and suffering.

William of St. Thierry (c. 1085–c. 1135). Belgian; Benedictine monk, abbot, friend of St. Bernard; reformer, mystic, spiritual writer.

Notes

Introduction: A Little Help From Our Friends

What the Holy Spirit: André Bessette, quoted in Henri-Paul Bergeron, *Brother André, the Wonder Man of Mount Royal,* Real Boudreau, trans. (Montreal: Fides, 1958), p. 136.

so that I...as joyful as: Henry Suso, *The Sister's Guide: The Letters of Henry Suso to His Spiritual Daughters,* Kathleen Goldmann, trans. (Springfield, Ill.: Templegate, 1955), pp. 31, 32.

Chapter One: Everyone's Invited

I was more...God is calling: Teresa of Avila, *The Life of Teresa of Jesus,* E. Allison Peers, trans. (Garden City, N.Y.: Doubleday Image, 1960), p. 112.

there is no one: Teresa of Avila, *Interior Castle,* E. Allison Peers, trans. (Garden City, N.Y.: Doubleday Image, 1961), p. 97.

All that the beginner: Teresa of Avila, *Castle,* Peers, p. 51.

For mental prayer: Teresa of Avila, *Life of St. Teresa, Written by Herself,* David Lewis, trans. (Westminster, Md.: Newman, 1948), p. 60.

All through our life: John Henry Newman, *Parochial and Plain Sermons* (London: Longmans, Green, 1891), vol. 7, pp. 23–24.

This Lord of ours: Teresa of Avila, *Castle,* Peers, p. 47.

We are not drawn: Francis de Sales, *Treatise on the Love of God,* H.B. Mackey, trans. (Westminster, Md.: Newman Bookshop, 1942), pp. 95–96.

Our good God: Jane Frances de Chantal, *St. Jane Frances Frémyot de Chantal: Her Exhortations, Conferences and Instructions,* Bristol Sisters of the Visitation trans. (Westminster, Md.: Newman Bookshop, 1947), p. 276.

And anyone who has not: Teresa of Avila, *Life,* Peers, trans., p. 110.

Oh, eternal wisdom: Suso, *Sister's Guide,* p. 22.

"I do not play": Catherine of Siena, *The Dialogue,* Suzanne Noffke, trans. (New York: Paulist, 1980), p. 116.

"prayer is primarily": Charles de Foucauld, *The Spiritual Autobiography of Charles de Foucauld,* Jean-François Six, ed., J. Holland Smith, trans. (Ijamsville, Md.: Word Among Us, 2003), p. 74.

I am surprised: Dorothy Day, *From Union Square to Rome* (Silver Spring, Md.: Preservation of the Faith Press, 1938), pp. 121–122.

You will become: Marie of the Incarnation, quoted in Fernand Jette, *The Spiritual Teaching of Mary of the Incarnation,* Mother M. Herman, trans. (New York: Sheed and Ward, 1963), p. 8.

Let us remember: Louise de Marillac, quoted in E.K. Saunders, ed., *Some Counsels of St. Vincent de Pault to which is appended the Thoughts of Mademoiselle LeGras* (London: Heath, Cranton and Ouseley, 1914), p. 141.

How shall they: Teresa of Avila, *The Way of Perfection,* A. Alexander, trans. (Cork: Mercier, 1936), pp. 130–133.

Love to pray: Mother Teresa of Calcutta, *A Gift for God: Prayers and Meditations* (New York: Harper and Row, 1975), p. 75.

He who perseveres: Elizabeth Seton, in Joseph B. Code, ed., *A Daily Thought from the Writings of Mother Seton* (Emmitsburg, Md.: Sisters of Charity of St. Vincent de Paul, 1929), entry for Feb. 2.

Dogged prayer: Gilbert of Hoyland, quoted in E. Scholl, *In the School of Love: An Anthology of Early Cistercian Texts* (Kalamazoo, Mich.: Cistercian, 2000), p. 88.

In your spiritual ascent: Albert the Great, *On Union with God* (New York: Continuum, 1911), p. 44.

Means for acquiring: Solanus Casey, quoted in Michael Crosby, *Solanus Casey: The Official Account of a Virtuous American Life* (New York: Crossroad, 2000), p. 44.

Pay unceasing attention: Charles de Foucauld, *Spiritual Autobiography,* p. 56.

"Can you not watch": Dorothy Day, *House of Hospitality* (New York: Sheed and Ward, 1939), pp. 131–132.

To fast: Elisabeth Leseur, *A Wife's Story: The Journal of Elizabeth Leseur* (London: Burns, Oates and Washbourne, 1921), p. 150.

Reflect on the everlasting love: Francis de Sales, *Introduction to the Devout Life,* John K. Ryan, trans. (New York: Doubleday Image, 1989), pp. 286–287.

Chapter Two: A Few Good Habits

If you are careful: Teresa of Avila, *The Way of Perfection,* E. Allison Peers, trans. (Garden City, N.Y.: Doubleday Image, 1964), p. 178.

The duties and cares: Edith Stein, *Essays on Woman,* vol. 2 of *The Collected Works of Edith Stein,* Freda Mary Oben, trans. (Washington, D.C.: ICS, 1987), vol. 2, pp. 130–131.

A little sprinkling: Peter of Alcantara, *Treatise on Prayer and Meditation,* Dominic Devas, trans. (Westminster, Md.: Newman, 1949), pp. 110–111.

We ought to have: Jerome, "Letter 22: To Eustochium," in *St. Jerome: Letters and Select Works,* vol. 6 of *A Select Library of Nicene and Post-Nicene Fathers of the Christian Church,* series 2, Philip Schaff and Henry Wace, eds. (New York: Christian Literature, 1890–1900), p. 38.

If you avoid: Thomas à Kempis, *The Imitation of Christ,* Leo Sherley-Price, trans. (N.Y.: Penguin, 1982), p. 50.

St. Teresa said: Alphonsus Liguori, *The Holy Eucharist,* vol. 6 of *The Complete Works of Saint Alphonsus de Liguori,* ed. Eugene Grimm, (Brooklyn, N.Y.: Redemptorist Fathers, 1934), p. 215.

Rise punctually: Vincent de Paul, *The Conferences of St. Vincent de Paul to the Sisters of Charity,* Joseph Leonard, trans. (Westminster, Md.: Newman, 1952), vol. 1, pp. 24, 28–29.

Thank and adore (my translation): Francis de Sales, *Introduction à la vie dévote* (Lyon: André Molin, 1820), pp. 116–118.

Our morning offering: Elizabeth Seton, quoted in Agnes Sadlier, *Elizabeth Seton: Her Life and Work* (Philadelphia: H.L. Kilner, 1905), pp.189–190.

During the activities: Jane Frances de Chantal, quoted in Peronne Marie Thibert, trans., *Francis de Sales and Jane de Chantal: Letters of Spiritual Direction* (Mahwah, N.J.: Paulist, 1988), pp. 301–302.

Each one must: Stein, pp. 131–132.

By the morning exercise (my translation): de Sales, *Vie dévote,* pp.110–120.

Source for "We thank God"?

Sunday is the property: John Vianney, *Instructions on the Catechism,* chap. 7. Available at www.ewtn.com/library.

How do you manage: François Trochu, *Saint Bernadette Soubirous,* John Joyce, trans. (Rockford, Ill.:Tan, 1985), p. 342.

The Catholic liturgy: Elisabeth Leseur, *Selected Writings of Elisabeth Leseur,* Janet Ruffing, ed. and trans. (Mahwah, N.J.: Paulist, 2005), p. 108.

Servants of God: Peter of Alcantara, p. 147.

A retreat: Leseur, *Wife's Story,* pp. 112–113.

You know how: John Paul II, *Prayers and Devotions from John Paul II,* Peter Canisius Johannes van Lierde, ed., Firman O'Sullivan, trans. (New York: Viking Penguin, 1994), p. 260.

It is spiritual solitude: Bernard of Clairvaux, *St. Bernard on the Song of Songs,* Religious of CSMV, trans. (London: A.R. Mowbray, 1952), p. 121.

Silence is the great: Père Jacques, quoted in Francis J. Murphy, *Père Jacques: Resplendent in Victory* (Washington, D.C.: ICS, 1998), p. 160.

How I wish: Thomas More, "The Sadness of Christ" in *The Tower Works: Devotional Writings,* G. Haupt, ed. (New Haven, Conn.: Yale University Press, 1980), p. 194.

Blessed are the nights (my translation): Charles de Foucauld, *Meditations sur les saints évangiles* (Paris: Montrouge: Nouvelle Cité, 1997), pp. 134, 135, 242–243.

What wife: Teresa of Avila, *Way,* Alexander, pp. 142–143.

Let us confess: Mark the Ascetic, quoted in E. Kadloubovsky and G.E.H. Palmer, trans. and eds., *Early Fathers from the Philokalia* (London: Faber and Faber, 1954), p. 74.

Chapter Three: A Question of Attitude

God detests...dear to God: Columba Marmion, *The English Letters of Columba Marmion, 1858–1923,* Gisbert Ghysens and Thomas Delforge, eds. (Baltimore: Helicon, 1962), p. 137.

an elevator: St. Thérèse of Lisieux, *Story of a Soul: The Autobiography of St. Thérèse of Lisieux,* John Clarke, trans. (Washington: ICS, 1996), p. 208.

When the Lord Jesus: Raymond of Capua, *The Life of St. Catherine of Siena,* trans. Conleth Kearns (Wilmington, Del.: Michael Glazier, 1980), p. 85.

O dearest Lord: Francis of Assisi, quoted in Johannes Jorgensen, *Francis of Assisi* (New York: Longmans, Green, 1912), pp. 296, 297.

While he stays: More, *Tower Works,* p. 208.

Why has God: Elizabeth of the Trinity, *Letters from Carmel,* vol. 2 of *The Complete Works of Elizabeth of the Trinity,* trans Anne Englund Nash (Washington, D.C.: ICS, 1995), p. 60.

In a flash: Marie of the Incarnation, *The Autobiography of Venerable Marie of the Incarnation, O.S.U.: Mystic and Missionary,* John J. Sullivan, trans. (Chicago: Loyola University Press, 1964), pp. 13–15.

My Jesus: Philip Neri, quoted in Jonathan Robinson, *Spiritual Combat Revisited* (San Francisco: Ignatius, 2003), p. 118.

This is all the grand science: Alphonsus Liguori, pp. 75–76.

It would be nothing: Claude de la Colombière, quoted in Georges Guitton, *Perfect Friend: The Life of Blessed Claude La Colombiere, S.J., 1641–1682,* William J. Young, trans. (St. Louis: Herder, 1956), p. 324.

Our imperfections: Francis de Sales, *Selected Letters,* Elisabeth Stopp, trans. (London: Faber & Faber, 1960), pp. 256–257.

Always turn: Vincent de Paul, *Counsels,* pp. 14–15.

Your failure: Solanus Casey, quoted in Crosby, p. 182.

Thérèse is weak: Thérèse of Lisieux, *Thoughts of Saint Thérèse,* Irish Carmelite, trans. (Rockford, Ill.: Tan, 1988), p. 41.

My God (my translation): Charles de Foucauld, quoted in Robert Claude and José Feder, eds., *Prie dans le secret: Recueil de prières* (Paris: Casterman, 1966), p. 196.

Don't be ever scrutinizing: Columba Marmion, *English Letters,* p. 185.

God has created: John Henry Newman, *Meditations and Devotions of the Late Cardinal Newman* (London: Longmans, Green, 1893), pp. 301–302.

Then I saw: Julian of Norwich, *Daily Readings with Julian of Norwich*, Robert Llewelyn, ed. (London: Darton, Longman and Todd, 1980), p. 5.

Prayers are always answered: Dorothy Day, *On Pilgrimage* (New York: Catholic Worker, 1948), entry for March 1973.

Let nothing disturb you: Teresa of Avila, quoted in John Kirvan, ed., *Let Nothing Disturb You* (Notre Dame, Ind.: Ave Maria, 1998), back cover.

Prayer and faith: Frances Cabrini, *The Travels of Mother Frances Xavier Cabrini, Foundress of the Missionary Sisters of the Sacred Heart of Jesus, as Related in Several of Her Letters* (Exeter, U.K.: Giovanni Serpentilli, 1925), pp. 69–70.

Chapter Four: But What Do You Say?

like a pleasant confidence: John Vianney, *Sermons for the Sundays and Feasts of the Year by the Curé of Ars* (New York: Joseph F. Wagner, 1901), p. 161.

Even toward little worms: Francis of Assisi, quoted in Marian A. Habig, ed., *St. Francis of Assisi: Writings and Early Biographies: English Omnibus of the Sources for the Life of St. Francis* (Cincinnati: St. Anthony Messenger Press, 2008), p. 296.

Most high: Francis of Assisi, adapted from Jorgensen, p. 314.

What a gift: Frances Cabrini, p. 121.

I set off: Elizabeth Seton, quoted in Leonard Feeney, *Mother Seton: Saint Elizabeth of New York* (Cambridge, Mass.: Ravengate, 1975), p. 84.

If only: Jane Frances de Chantal, *St. Chantal on Prayer*, A. Durand, trans. (Boston: St. Paul, 1968), p. 28.

I come: Gertrude the Great of Helfta, *Spiritual Exercises*, Gertrud Jaron Lewis and Jack Lewis, trans. (Kalamazoo, Mich.: Cistercian, 1989), p. 67.

You are here (my translation): Charles de Foucauld, quoted in Claude and Feder, p. 136.

Let us thank: Solanus Casey, quoted in Catherine M. Odell, *Father Solanus: The Story of Solanus Casey* (Huntington, Ind.: Our Sunday Visitor, 1988), pp. 214–215.

Know that: Frances Cabrini, p. 82.

Do you not perceive: Bernard of Clairvaux, *On the Song of Songs I*, vol. 2 of *The Works of Bernard of Clairvaux*, Kilian Walsh, trans. (Kalamazoo, Mich.: Cistercian, 1981), pp. 88, 89.

John Damascene: Thomas Aquinas, *The Three Greatest Prayers* (Manchester, N.H.: Sophia, 1990), p. 102.

I can state: Augustine, "Letter 130: To Proba," in *The Confessions and Letters of*

St. Augustine, vol. 1 of *Nicene and Post-Nicene Fathers*, series 1, Philip Schaff, ed., p. 462.

A soul rises up: Catherine of Siena, pp. 25–26.

"My daughter": Faustina Kowalska, *Divine Mercy in My Soul: Diary of St. Maria Faustina Kowalska* (Stockbridge, Mass.: Marian, 2008), p. 629.

You don't need: Macarius the Great, quoted in Benedicta Ward, *Sayings of the Desert Fathers: The Alphabetical Collection* (Kalamazoo, Mich.: Cistercian, 1975), p. 111.

Speak to him: Peter Julian Eymard, quoted in A. Tesnière, *St. Peter Julian Eymard, the Priest of the Eucharist* (New York: Eymard League, 1962), pp. 109–110.

You wrote: Josemaría Escrivá de Balaguer, *The Way* (London: Scepter, 1979), no. 91, p. 39.

Let your prayer: John Climacus, *The Ladder of Divine Ascent*, as quoted in M. Basil Pennington, *Centering Prayer* (New York: Doubleday/Image, 1980), pp. 41–42.

However quietly: Teresa of Avila, *Way*, Peers, trans., p. 184.

For me: Thérèse of Lisieux, *Thoughts*, p. 121.

You have undoubtedly: Père Jacques, quoted in Murphy, p. 165.

When you feel: Columba Marmion, *English Letters*, p. 172.

Thus I said: Marie of the Incarnation, *Marie of the Incarnation: Selected Writings*, Irene Mahoney, ed. (New York: Paulist, 1989), p. 215.

Chapter Five: The Book That Comes Alive

with much toil: Jerome, "Letter 108: To Eustochium," p. 209.

ignorance of the Scriptures: Jerome, *Commentariorum in Isaiam libri xviii*, prol.: PL 24, 17b, as quoted in *Catechism of the Catholic Church* #133.

Jesus concealed: Jerome, "Letter 53: To Paulinus," p. 98.

Whose disciple: Bert Ghezzi, *Voices of the Saints: A Year of Readings* (New York: Doubleday, 2000), pp. 336–337.

Anyone who thirsts: Bernard of Clairvaux, quoted in Scholl, p. 84.

Good Lord: Thomas More, *Prayers of St. Thomas More and Treatise on the Holy Eucharist* (London: Burns, Oates and Washbourne, 1938), p. 26.

All sacred scriptures: Thomas à Kempis, p. 33.

He would sit: Dominic, *Saint Dominic: Biographical Documents*, Francis C. Lehner, ed. (Washington, D.C.: Thomist, 1964), pp. 157–158.

Our meditations: Bernard of Clairvaux, *On the Song of Songs II*, vol. 3 of *The Works of Bernard of Clairvaux*, Kilian Walsh, trans. (Kalamazoo, Mich.: Cistercian, 1976), p. 137.

a bit sad (my translation): Thérèse de Lisieux, *Carnet Jaune* in *Oeuvres complètes de Thérèse de Lisieux* (Paris: Editions du Cerf, 1992), p. 1002.

Read often: Jerome, "Letter 29: To Eustochium," pp. 28, 32.

The farther I go: Leseur, *Wife's Story*, p. 52.

To keep the thought: John Cassian, *John Cassian: Conferences,* Colm Luibheid, trans. (New York: Paulist, 1985), pp. 132–133.

I would try: Teresa of Avila, *Life*, Lewis, p. 66.

Lord, I believe: Dorothy Day, *On Pilgrimage,* July–August 1973, Dorothy Day Library. Available at www.catholicworker.org/dorothyday.

I am the lost sheep: John XXIII, *Journal of a Soul*, Dorothy White, trans. (New York: McGraw-Hill, 1965), pp. 68–69.

Often when: Elizabeth Seton, quoted in Charles White, *Life of Mrs. Eliza A. Seton, Foundress and First Superior of the Sisters or Daughters of Charity in the United States of America* (New York: P.J. Kennedy, 1879), pp. 71, 143, 154.

If the psalm: Augustine, *The Teaching of St. Augustine on Prayer and the Contemplative Life,* Hugh Pope, trans. (London: Burns, Oates and Washbourne, 1935), p. 2.

In the psalms: Marie of the Incarnation, *Writings*, pp. 101–102.

I am easily: Frederic Ozanam, quoted in Kathleen O'Meara, *Life and Works of Frederic Ozanam* (New York: Catholic Truth Publishing Society, 1883), p. 333.

I'm always encouraging (translation by Kevin Perrotta): John Chrysostom, "Seven Homilies on Lazarus," in J.P. Migne, *Patrologiae Graecae* (Paris: n.p., 1862), homily 3, vol. 48, pp. 991–993.

I read the opening: St. Ephrem the Syrian, hymns 5 and 6, *Hymns on Paradise*, Sebastian Brock, trans. (Crestwood, N.Y.: St. Vladimir's Seminary Press, 1990), pp. 103, 109.

Chapter Six: What to Do With Your Mind

nothing other than: Francis de Sales, "The Goal of Prayer," in *Sermons on Prayer,* available at www.theworkofGod.org.

Since prayer places: Francis de Sales, *Devout Life*, Ryan, p. 81.

My only goal: Anthony Mary Claret, *Autobiography*, José María Viñas, ed. and trans. (Chicago: Claretian, 1976), pp. 20–21.

It happens: Teresa of Avila, *The Way of Perfection* in *Collected Works of St. Teresa of Avila*, Kavanaugh and Rodriguez, trans. (Washington, D.C.: ICS, 1980), vol. 2, p. 156.

Although our outward aspect: Nilus of Sinai, quoted in Kadloubovsky and Palmer, *Early Fathers from the Philokalia*, pp. 145–146.

That blessed rosary: John XXIII, p. 76.

My God: John Henry Newman, *Meditations and Devotions*, p. 328.

I do not say: Teresa of Avila, *The Interior Castle or the Mansions*, Discalced Carmelite, trans. (London: Sands, 1945), p. 9.

To mutter: Francis de Sales, "The Kinds of Prayer" in *Sermons*.

The practice: Br. Lawrence of the Resurrection, *Writings and Conversations on the Practice of the Presence of God,* Conrad De Meester, ed., Salvatore Sciurba, trans. (Washington, D.C.: ICS, 1994), p. 39.

How are we: Vincent de Paul, *Counsels*, p. 79.

The first consists (my translation): Francis de Sales, *Vie dévote*, pp. 96–99.

Prayer consists: St. Bonaventure ("On the Perfection of Life"), as quoted in Pennington, p. 45.

We picture Jesus (my translation): Jane Frances de Chantal, "Entretien 32," in *Sainte Jeanne-Françoise Frémyot de Chantal, sa vie et ses oeuvres* (Paris: Plon, 1909), vol. 2, pp. 331–332.

The first point: Ignatius of Loyola, *The Spiritual Exercises of St. Ignatius,* Anthony Mottola, trans. (Garden City, N.Y.: Doubleday Image, 1964), p. 72.

After offering myself: Br. Lawrence, *Writings,* p. 75.

Let us imagine: Teresa of Avila, *Way*, Kavanaugh and Rodriguez, trans., pp. 143–144.

We can consider (my translation): Jane Frances de Chantal, "Entretien 32."

I wish that: Paul of the Cross, letter of April 8, 1758. Available at www.passionists.com.

One may sit or kneel: Ignatius of Loyola, *Spiritual Exercises of Saint Ignatius: A Translation and Commentary*, George Ganss, trans. (Chicago: Loyola, 1992), pp. 180–181.

If you find: Claude de la Colombière, quoted in Guitton, p. 335.

Always prepare: Marie of the Incarnation, quoted in Jette, pp. 81–82.

Meditation is the mother: Francis de Sales, "Goal of Prayer," *Sermons.*

Chapter Seven: Struggles and Snags

ordinarily nothing: Jane Frances de Chantal, quoted in Elisabeth Stopp, *Madame de Chantal: Portrait of a Saint* (Westminster, Md.: Newman, 1963), p. 233.

Don't fear them: Francis de Sales, *Letters to Persons in the World*, H.B. Mackey, trans. (Surrey, B.C.: Eremitical, 2010), pp. 188–189.

Do you know: Jane Frances de Chantal, *Selected Letters of St. Jane Frances de Chantal*, Sisters of the Visitation, trans. (London: Washbourne and Oates, 1918), pp. 2010.

I consider her: Vincent de Paul, quoted in Stopp, p. 233.

Leave at the door: Alphonsus Liguori, p. 273.

One Lent: Thomas of Celano, in Francis of Assisi, *Writings*, p. 442.

The very pains: Jane Frances de Chantal, *St. Chantal on Prayer*, pp. 60–61.

Who would put up with: Augustine, *Prayer*, p. 36.

As regards prayer: Francis de Sales, *The Art of Loving God* (Manchester, N.H.: Sophia, 1998), p. 86.

The whole aim: Teresa of Avila, *Castle*, Carmelite, p. 19.

Oh, the great illusion: Claude de la Colombière, quoted in Guitton, p. 325.

There are people: Jane Frances de Chantal, quoted in *Live Jesus! Wisdom from Saints Francis de Sales and Jane de Chantal*, Louise Perrotta, ed. (Ijamsville, Md.: Word Among Us, 2000), pp. 85–86.

Pray out loud: (my translation) Francis de Sales, *Vie dévote*, pp. 113–115.

Sometimes when I find: Thérèse of Lisieux, *Thoughts*, p. 121.

Whenever you go: (my translation) Mary Euphrasia Pelletier, quoted in Charles-Louis Portais, *La Servante de Dieu, Marie de Saint-Euphrasie Pelletier*, vol. 2 (Paris: Delhomme et Briguet, 1893), p. 330.

If the tediousness: Alphonsus Liguori, p. 282.

In meditation, prayer: Elizabeth Seton, quoted in Sadlier, p. 170.

but this trouble: John of the Cross, *Dark Night of the Soul*, E. Allison Peers, trans. (New York: Doubleday Image, 1959), pp. 69–71.

I thank my Jesus: Thérèse of Lisieux, *Thoughts*, p. 59.

Therefore during this time: Claude de la Colombière, *The Spiritual Direction of Saint Claude de la Colombière*, Mother M. Philip, trans. (San Francisco: Ignatius, 1998), p. 59.

They think my faith: Mother Teresa, *Come Be My Light*, Brian Kolodiejchuk, ed. (New York: Random House, 2007), pp. 187–188.

I have come: Mother Teresa of Calcutta, *Come Be My Light*, p. 214.

My soul has longed: Henry Suso, quoted in Angela Ashwin, *The Book of a Thousand Prayers* (Grand Rapids, Mich.: Zondervan, 2002), p. 272.

Often during: Catherine of Siena, p. 122.

When the enemy: Thérèse of Lisieux, *Thoughts*, p. 32.

If sleeping: Vincent de Paul, *Conferences*, vol. 1, p. 29.

The devil: Alphonsus Liguori, pp. 61–63.

Never abandon prayer: Vincent de Paul, *Conferences*, vol. 2, pp. 55, 56.

Chapter Eight: Try This

Nine Ways of Prayer: Dominic, quotes and information from pp. 149–157.

If you want: Augustine, *Prayer*, p. 49.

Fasting gives us: Bernard of Clairvaux, *St. Bernard's Sermons for the Seasons and Principal Festivals of the Year,* a Priest of Mount Melleray, trans. (Westminster, Md.: Carroll, 1950), vol. 2, p. 90.

For Scripture says: Angela Merici, quoted in Sr. M. Monica, *Angela Merici and Her Teaching Idea* (London: Longmans, Green, 1927), p. 251.

He who wishes: Philip Neri, quoted in Alfonso Capecelatro, *The Life of Saint Philip Neri* (London: Burns & Oates, 1882), vol. 1, p. 429.

Prayer knocks: St. Peter Chrysologus, quoted in *Touching the Risen Christ: Wisdom from the Fathers* (Ijamsville, Md.: Word Among Us, 1999), p. 27.

Imagine that this Lord: Teresa of Avila, *Way,* Peers, p. 173.

Imagine Christ: Ignatius of Loyola, *Exercises,* Mottola, p. 56.

I talked and prayed: Anthony Mary Claret, p. 15.

Have in your hands: Vincent de Paul, *Conferences,* vol. 2, pp. 56–57; vol. 4, p. 189.

Try to carry: Teresa of Avila, *Way,* Kavanaugh and Rodriguez, trans., p. 136.

Oh, how many times: Teresa of Avila, *The Book of My Life,* Mirabai Starr, trans. (Boston: New Seeds, 2007), p. 236.

He greatly enjoyed: Ignatius of Loyola, *A Pilgrim's Journey. Autobiography of Ignatius of Loyola,* Joseph Tylenda, ed. and trans. (Collegeville, Minn.: Liturgical, 1985), pp. 16–17.

I shall meditate: Dorothy Day, *House of Hospitality,* p. 2.

You don't know: Josemaría Escrivá, p. 40.

We are not sufficiently: Frederic Ozanam, quoted in O'Meara, pp. 327, 328.

My Jesus: Philip Neri, quoted in Ponnelle and Bordet, *St. Philip Neri and His Times* (London: Sheed and Ward, 1932), selected from pp. 596–597.

There is nothing: Augustine, *Prayer,* pp. 28–29.

Some teach: Gregory of Sinai, quoted in E. Kadloubovsky and G.E.H. Palmer, trans. and eds., *Writings from the Philokalia on Prayer of the Heart* (London: Faber and Faber, 1951), p. 74.

Haphazard reading: William of St. Thierry, *The Golden Epistle,* Theodore Berkeley, trans. (Spencer, Mass.: Cistercian, 1971), pp. 51–52.

We owe much: Alphonsus de Orozco, quoted in Kathleen Pond, *The Spirit of the Spanish Mystics* (London: Burns and Oates, 1958), p. 52.

Be certain that if: John Gabriel Perboyre, quoted in G. de Montgesty, *Two Vincentian Martyrs* (Maryknoll, N.Y.: Catholic Foreign Mission Society of America, 1925), p. 123.

People who try: Francis de Sales, *Art of Loving God,* p. 94.

Chapter Nine: Prayer's Best Teacher

I am the mortal enemy: Columba Marmion, *English Letters*, p. 126.

Don't suppose: Francis de Sales, quoted in Charles Dollen, *Fire of Love* (St. Louis: Herder, 1964), p. 87.

Be humble: Philip Neri, quoted in V.J. Matthews, *St. Philip Neri* (Rockford, Ill.: Tan, 1984), p. 71.

I have a great desire: Columba Marmion, quoted in Dollen, p. 8.

St. Paul tells us: Columba Marmion, *Christ the Ideal of the Monk* (St. Louis: Herder, 1926), p. 123.

You may perhaps say: Columba Marmion, *Christ in His Mysteries* (St. Louis: Herder, 1939), p. 124.

The Holy Spirit: Père Jacques, quoted in Murphy, pp. 164–165.

disciple of the Holy Spirit: Louise de Marillac. Quotes and following information from Jean Calvet, *Louise de Marillac: A Portrait* (New York: P.J. Kenedy, 1959), pp. 179–181.

It is this Holy Spirit: Columba Marmion, *Christ, the Ideal of the Priest* (St. Louis: Herder, 1952), p. 303.

The Holy Spirit is: Philip Neri, quoted in Paul Turks, *Philip Neri: The Fire of Joy* (New York: Alba House, 1995), p. 122.

I think that (my translation)*:* Elisabeth Leseur, *Lettres sur la souffrance*, F. Leseur, ed. (Paris: de Gigord, 1927), pp. 184–185.

The great method: Jane Frances de Chantal, *Live Jesus!*, pp. 135–136.

For each one: Ignatius of Loyola, quoted in Dollen, p. 86.

We can, like our Lord: Charles de Foucauld, *Spiritual Meditations on Faith*, Alexandra Russell, trans. (New York: New City, 1988), p. 78.

Let us now consider: Bernard of Clairvaux, *Sermons*, vol. 2, pp. 291–292.

In every soul: Columba Marmion, *English Letters,* p. 140.

I recommend you: Columba Marmion, *English Letters,* p. 141.

Let us be faithful: Frances Cabrini, pp. 41–42.

If only we would: Francis de Sales, *The Love of God, a Treatise,* Vincent Kerns, trans. (Westminster, Md.: Newman, 1962), pp. 76–77.

What the Holy Spirit: André Bessette, quoted in Bergeron, p. 136.

Wherever people are praying: John Paul II, *Go in Peace: A Gift of Enduring Love,* Joseph Durepos, ed. (Chicago: Loyola, 2003), pp. 9–10.

When we are faithful: Columba Marmion, *Christ the Life of the Soul,* Nuns of Tyburn Convent, trans. (London: Sands, 1928), pp. 316–317.

God grants it: Vincent de Paul, *Counsels,* p. 85.

I was only twenty: Marie of the Incarnation, *Autobiography,* p. 16.

Our Lord started: Charles of Sezze, *Autobiography,* trans. Leonard Perotti

(London: Catholic Book Club, 1963), p. 17.

I have prayed: Anthony the Great, quoted in Kadloubovsky and Palmer, *Early Fathers from the Philokalia*, pp. 45–46.

If you desire: Frances Cabrini, p. 81.

O you who are: William of St. Thierry, *On Contemplating God*, Sr. Penelope, trans. (Spencer, Mass.: Cistercian, 1971), p. 58.

Chapter Ten: Pray Your Way Through the Day

The remembrance of Jesus: John Climacus, *The Ladder of Divine Ascent* (New York: Paulist, 1982), p. 48.

simple attention: Lawrence of the Resurrection. Quotes and information from *Walking with the Father: Wisdom from Brother Lawrence* (Ijamsville, Md.: Word Among Us, 1999), pp. 7, 10, 28, 29, 34, 39.

remind ourselves: Francis de Sales, *Devout Life*, p. 90.

Those words: Josemaría Escrivá, p. 41.

The good thoughts: Vincent de Paul, quoted in Frances Ryan and John E. Rybolt, eds. *Vincent de Paul and Louise de Marillac: Rules, Conferences, and Writings* (New York: Paulist, 1995), p. 203.

Keep silence: Francis de Sales, *Introduction to the Devout Life*, Joseph Bowler and Lewis Fiorelli, trans. (Rockford, Ill.: Tan), pp. 69–71.

By an impulse: Raymond of Capua, *Life*, pp. 46–47.

We can meditate: Alponsus Liguori, pp. 268–272.

Isn't that simple: Elizabeth of the Trinity, *I Have Found God: Letters from Carmel*, in *Complete Works*, Anne Englund North, trans. (Washington, D.C.: ICS Publications, 1995), vol. 2, pp. 215–216.

God does not ask: Br. Lawrence, *Practice,* pp. 69–70.

For instance: Elizabeth Seton, quoted in Joseph I. Dirvin, *Mrs. Seton, Foundress of the American Sisters of Charity* (New York: Farrar, Straus and Giroux, 1975), p. 182.

Alas: Henry Suso, *Sister's Guide*, p. 20.

Try to have: Vincent de Paul, *Counsels,* pp. 108, 109–110.

Go and find God: Jeanne Jugan, quoted in Gabriel Marie Garronne, *Poor in Spirit: Awaiting All from God* (London: Darton, Longman, and Todd, 1975), p. 71.

Then the rest of the day: Edith Stein, quoted in Waltraud Herbstrith, *Edith Stein: A Biography* (San Francisco: Harper and Row, 1971), p. 54.

We went into: Edith Stein, Herbstrith, p. 29.

Let's try not: Alphonsus Liguori, p. 281.

How can I: Vincent de Paul, *Conferences*, selected from pp. 202–205.

At night: Bernadette, quoted in Trochu, pp. 344–345.

I have personally: Anthony Mary Claret, p. 115.

Blessed voice: Frances Cabrini, pp. 49–50.

In her imagination: Raymond of Capua, *Life*, pp. 47–48.

I remember: Marie of the Incarnation, quoted in Jette, pp. 89–90.

A brief lifting: Br. Lawrence, *Practice*, p. 63.

A good way: Francis de Sales, "The Heart of Prayer," *Sermons.*

We must pray: Elizabeth Seton, quoted in Dirvin, pp. 181–182.

Let no one think: Gregory Palamas, quoted in Kadloubovsky and Palmer, *Early Fathers from the Philokalia*, pp. 412–413.

Whatever the object: William of St. Thierry, *Contemplating*, p. 117.

Chapter Eleven: One Big Prayer Chain: The Communion of Saints

little Mary Harrington…had told me: Brigid O'Shea Merriman, *Searching for Christ: The Spirituality of Dorothy Day* (Notre Dame, Ind.: University of Notre Dame Press, 1994), p. 173.

new companions: Merriman, pp. 174–175.

even closer: Merriman, note 2, p. 285.

One day: Jim Forest, "Dorothy Day—A Saint for Our Age?" (from a talk given at Marquette University on October 2, 1997), Available at the Dorothy Day Library (www.catholicworker.org/dorothyday).

the authors whose names: Philip Neri, quoted in Matthews, p. 71.

indulging in…I used to find: Teresa of Avila. Quotes and information drawn from Teresa of Avila, *Life*, Peers, trans., pp. 96, 117–118.

This is the truth: Edith Stein, quoted in Herbstrith, pp. 64–65, 70.

I'm reading (my translation): Elisabeth Leseur, *Lettres*, pp. 235–236.

While reading: Ignatius of Loyola, *Autobiography*, pp. 13–14.

Right now (my translation): Frederic Ozanam, *Lettres de Frederic Ozanam* in *Oeuvres complètes* (Paris: Jacques Lecoffre, 1865), vol. 10, p. 266.

my teacher: Anthony Mary Claret, p. 166.

For if it is lawful: Alphonsus Liguori, p. 35.

And I ask my Savior: Elizabeth Seton, in *The Soul of Elizabeth Seton* (New York: Benziger Brothers, 1936), pp. 44–45.

May the virgin: Pio of Pietrelcina, quoted in Alessio Parente, *Our Lady of Grace Prayer Book* (San Giovanni Rotondo, Italy: Our Lady of Grace Capuchin Friary, 1988), p. 189.

I took for my advocate: Teresa of Avila, *Life*, Peers, trans., pp. 93–94.

if they were…O my loving: John XXIII, p. 110.

Imagine yourselves: Philip Neri, quoted in Capecelatro, p. 411.

Prayer: Anthony Mary Claret, p. 94.

I rose at three: Peter Favre, quoted in William V. Bangert, *The Life of Blessed Peter Favre: First Companion of St. Ignatius* (San Francisco: Ignatius, 2002).

God's conquest (my translation): Elisabeth Leseur. Quotes and information selected from Leseur, *Wife's Story,* pp. 53, 172; also *Lettres,* 137–138, 147–148.

I consider: Dorothy Day, "Reflections During Advent, 4: Obedience," *Ave Maria* (December 17, 1966), p. 23.

I'm so sorry…Poor Holy Father: Jacinta Marto, quoted in Leo Madigan, *The Children of Fatima: Blessed Francisco and Blessed Jacinta Marto* (Huntington, Ind.: Our Sunday Visitor, 2003), pp. 247, 248, 135.

I would like to celebrate: John Paul II, "Homily for the Beatification of Francisco and Jacinta Marto," May 13, 2000 (www.vatican.va).

Almighty and tender Lord: Anselm, *The Prayers and Meditations of St. Anselm,* Benedicta Ward, trans. (New York: Penguin, 1973), pp. 216, 217, 219.

Never cease offering: Catherine of Siena, pp. 159–160.

Chapter Twelve: It's All About Love

Abbot Lot: Adapted from Helen Waddell, *The Desert Fathers* (New York: Vintage, 1998), p. 117.

While I was about to go: Veronica Giuliani, quoted in Michael L. Gaudoin-Parker, *A Window on the Mystery of Faith: Mystical Umbria Enlivened by the Eucharist* (New York: Alba, 1997), as quoted in Bert Ghezzi, *Voices of the Saints: A Year of Readings* (New York: Doubleday, 2000), p. 716.

To love Jesus: Thomas à Kempis, pp. 91–92.

O infinite goodness: Teresa of Avila, *Life,* Lewis, pp. 60–61.

It is through prayer: John Paul II, *Prayers and Devotions,* pp. 261–262.

We cannot see: Père Jacques, quoted in Murphy, p. 154.

By such prayer: Catherine of Siena, p. 25.

Abide in me: Elizabeth of the Trinity, quoted in M.M. Philipon, *The Spiritual Doctrine of Sister Elizabeth of the Trinity,* a Benedictine of Stanbrook Abbey, trans. (Westminster, Md.: Newman Bookshop, 1947), p. 220.

Prayer unites: Julian of Norwich, *Julian of Norwich: Showings,* Edmund Colledge and James Walsh, trans. (New York: Paulist, 1978), pp. 253, 254.

Place your mind: Clare of Assisi, in *Francis and Clare: The Complete Works,* Regis Armstrong and Ignatius Brady, trans. (New York: Paulist, 1982), pp. 9–14.

Night and morning: John Vianney, *Sermons,* p. 248.

Extend your love: Augustine, quoted in Benedict J. Groeschel, *Augustine: Major Writings* (New York: Crossroad, 1996), p. 159.

When I see people: Teresa of Avila, *Castle*, Peers, p. 116.

My Jesus: Faustina Kowalska, p. 449.

When I began: Charles of Sezze, p. 19.

We have been sent: Vincent de Paul, *Counsels,* pp. 32, 34.

Prayer is powerful: Frances Cabrini, pp. 166–167.

O God, love: Gertrude the Great, pp. 91–92.

Give me the grace: Philip Neri, quoted in Ponnelle and Bordet, pp. 596–597.

O you who have willed: William of St. Thierry, *Contemplating*, p. 190.